UFL

Collective Bargaining Agreement

Louis Marino, PhD
Brandy Booth
John Garrett
John Hataway
Jeremy Haynie
Donald Maginnis
Leslie Scarbrough
Kristen Smith
Wes Stoddard

The University of Alabama

Editor in Chief: David Parker
Acquisitions Editor: Michael Ablassmeir
Assistant Editor: Denise Vaughn
Associate Director, Manufacturing: Vincent Scelta
Buyer: Michelle Klein
Printer/Binder: Bind-Rite Graphics
Cover Printer: Phoenix / Hagerstown

Pearson Prentice HallTM is a trademark of Pearson Education, Inc.

PEARSON
Prentice
Hall

10   9   8   7   6   5   4   3   2   1

ISBN-13: 978-0-13-158766-3
ISBN-10:   0-13-158766-8

TABLE OF CONTENTS

UFL Negotiation Goals and Purpose

The importance of collective bargaining and negotiations is often emphasized in management classes without providing a real-world example that can make the negotiation process accessible to students. With the prevalence of negotiation breakdown in professional sports (NFL, MLB, NHL, etc.) and the ensuing lock-outs and strikes that result, the United Football League's (UFL) collective bargaining agreement provides a clear example of successful negotiations between a management group and a collective bargaining group in the world of professional sports.

This case study is based upon, but is not an exact reproduction of, the previous collective bargaining agreements between the National Football League Players Association (NFLPA) and the NFL owners' group. Each participant in this negotiation will represent either an owner in the UFL owners group, or an UFLPA union representative.

Participants in this negotiation will utilize both integrative and distributive negotiation techniques as they strive to reach an agreement amongst themselves and with the opposing group. Taken individually, the majority of the negotiation issues in this case are distributive in nature, with each side attempting to maximize their personal outcomes. However, both teams must remember that the success of the league determines, to an extent, individual success. This means that the negotiation as a whole should be viewed as an integrative bargaining situation in which the success of the UFL as a whole will determine the success of each individual group.

In the course of this negotiation, you will be required to apply the tactics learned in the classroom to an environment that will closely model negotiations that you might encounter in the workplace. The combination of integrative and distributive bargaining techniques employed in this negotiation will prepare you for the complex negotiations that can take place both within and between companies in today's work environment.

General History

The Evolution of American Football

The sport that has become known as American football began sometime during the 19th century in England. A soccer player, tired of using only his feet to maneuver the ball, decided to pick up the ball and run with it. This was illegal in soccer of course, but the new style caught on with players and a new sport called rugby was born.

Rugby became a global success and reached the United States in the mid-1800s, where it became a popular sport on the campuses of the nation's elite universities. The first intercollegiate game was played on November 6, 1869, in New Brunswick, New Jersey, between in-state rivals Princeton and Rutgers. In 1873, representatives from Columbia, Cornell, Yale, and a few other colleges met to form the Intercollegiate Football Association and to adopt a common code. Harvard University, whose team insisted on playing the "Boston Game," a cross between soccer and rugby, did not participate in the IFA meeting. As teams played Harvard and adapted to its version of the game, they found that they preferred the "Boston Game" and in 1876 representatives from Harvard, Yale, Princeton, and Columbia met to form a new Intercollegiate Football Association based on the rugby rules.

The game evolved further through the efforts of Walter Camp. Camp played football for Yale in 1876-1881 and, beginning in 1878, played a crucial role on the Rules Committee for three decades. Two of Camp's rules – the decision to award possession of the ball to one of the two teams, and the rule that a team must advance the ball 5 yards or lose ten in three downs (plays) or it would be obliged to surrender the ball to the other side – were instrumental in shaping the game known today. For his efforts, Camp is recognized as the "Father of American Football."

College football's popularity grew rapidly in the United States. Fans not only loved the sport, but the bands, cheerleaders, pep rallies, and alumni reunions that surrounded the sport. The game was temporarily put on hold for World War I, but surged back in the 1920s and became widely recognized as America's greatest sporting spectacle. By the end of the decade, three networks were broadcasting a variety of games and local stations were covering their home teams, newsreel companies were devoting 20-25 percent of their footage to football in the fall, and popular magazines such as Collier's and the Saturday Evening Post regularly published articles about football.

In the 1920s and 1930s, colleges and universities throughout the United States began organizing conferences to gain recognition for their football programs. Bowl games also emerged to provide opportunities for interregional play, as well as to create a profitable commercial enterprise. So many bowl games emerged that the NCAA stepped in to regulate them in 1950.

The American Professional Football Association began in 1920 with 14 teams, and changed its name to the National Football Association in 1922. Joe Carr, an experienced promoter, became president of the NFL in 1921 and remained in this position until his death in 1939. The organization took its modern shape under Carr when it was organized into two five-team divisions whose leaders would meet in a championship game at the end of the season. The teams were all from large cities, with the exception of Green Bay, Wisconsin. The sport became popular in cities where teams were based, but still had trouble competing with the rivalries, enthusiasm, and pageantry of college football.

In the 1920s, University of Illinois player Red Grange became college football's first true celebrity. His performances in games against Michigan and Pennsylvania earned him national acclaim. But, he also gained notoriety in 1925 for leaving Illinois without graduating to play professional football for the Chicago Bears of the United Football League. This was one of the first incidents of professionalism (paying coaches, recruiting and subsidizing athletes, commercializing the game) in football, a controversial issue disliked by college administrations but ignored by the public and sportswriters who embraced the sport.

Professionalism was widely regarded as the greatest threat to college football, and made professional football less respectable in the public eye. Red Grange's turning professional created a temporary boost to the professional game, but the league still had trouble maintaining interest outside their franchises' cities. This problem would soon be solved by the emergence of a new technology called television.

In the 1950s, the introduction of television helped professional football reach beyond its franchise cities to become a national sport. The medium became increasingly lucrative for the sport and produced television contracts that created large profits for every team despite their record. NFL Commissioner Bert Bell embraced television immediately and even won congressional approval to black-out television broadcasts of games in cities where the home team was playing. This assured strong attendance for the team and had little effect on the size of the sport's rapidly growing television audience.

After his death in 1959, Bell was succeeded by the general manager of the Los Angeles Rams, Pete Rozelle, who became recognized as the most powerful and most effective commissioner in American professional sports. Rozelle negotiated a series or contract with television networks which grew from $4.65 million for the 1962 season to nearly $500 million per year when he retired in 1989. This generated tremendous profit for the NFL and its teams, guaranteeing more than $17 million to each club before a single ticket was sold. Additionally, Rozelle persuaded Congress to continue exemption of the NFL from the Sherman Antitrust Act, allowing franchises to operate not as individual businesses but single entities and share equally in the league-generated revenues. Rozelle's leadership increased the value of the franchises from about $1 million in 1960 to more than $100 million in 1989, and under the structure he established, franchise values exceeded $500 million by the end of the 20th century.

Many leagues had attempted to form to compete with the NFL, but none posed a significant threat until the American Football League formed in 1960. Backed by Texas billionaire Lamar Hunt, the AFL fielded teams in eight cities, including three with NFL franchises. The AFL landed a television contract with NBC, giving it more power and security than its predecessors.

The NFL and the AFL agreed to a merger in 1966. The merger was completed in 1970 and resulted in twenty-six clubs and the creation of the Super Bowl, which would soon become the most popular and lucrative sporting event in the United States. The first Super Bowl was played between the Green Bay Packers and the Kansas City Chiefs after the 1966 season. More than 40 percent of the nation's televisions were tuned to the two networks that covered the event, and the spectacle eventually came to be watched by as many as 130 million Americans, in addition to a worldwide audience. The Super Bowl became a major civic event and part of American culture.

In the early 1970s, polls began to repeatedly identify professional football as America's favorite sport. The NFL withstood challenges from new rivals such as the World Football League (1974-75), the United States Football League (1983-85) and Arena Football. By the turn of the 21st century, professional football was considered by far the most popular and most profitable of all American sports.

Off the field, the NFL was shaped by two major legal decisions. First, free agency became an option for players in 1993 after a series of lawsuits and disputes. Problems began when players, realizing the tremendous growth of television revenues, demanded a fair share of the profits. In 1970, the NFL Players Association instigated a brief training camp strike, followed by a 41-day strike in 1974 during training camp. More serious strikes occurred in 1982 and 1987, causing damage to the league's reputation and resulting in an unsuccessful outcome for the players. After the 1993 free agency decision was made, players were able to change teams and their salaries increased dramatically. However, a salary cap was imposed to maintain the clubs' financial stability and competitive balance.

Another legal decision that impacted the league was the decision to allow owners to move their franchises without league approval. This began in 1980 when Al Davis, managing general partner of the Oakland Raiders, successfully sued the NFL for not allowing him to move his team to Los Angeles, where he expected to earn greater profits (he later moved the team back to Oakland in 1995). This decision gave owners more power with local governments and provoked local outrage as numerous franchises changed locations in the 1980s and 90s.

A Brief History of Collective Bargaining Agreements in the NFL

The current NFL Collective Bargaining Agreement (CBA) between the players and the owners is directly tied to the 1982 agreement that came about as a result of a player strike during the 1982 season. Since the strike, the two parties have shown a strong willingness to work with each other to prevent a repeat of that work stoppage. There was even a period of several years in the late eighties and early nineties where no collective bargaining agreement was agreed upon. The 1993 agreement that ended this period serves as the core of all of the agreements since. Each of the agreements since 1993 has been an extension of the prior agreement with a few amendments and additions.

The roots of the NFL collective bargaining agreements go back as far as 1956 when the NFL Players Association was founded. The first major agreement, however, came in 1970 after the NFL and AFL merged under the NFL name. The terms of the first CBA included agreements about pension contributions, per diem payments for preseason games, and disability fund contributions. This agreement lasted until a new agreement was formed in 1977.

The 1977 CBA brought several new issues into the mix. It increased the league's pension contribution to an average of $11 million per year over its five year life, a notable increase from the $4.35 million annual contribution under the old agreement. Insurance and benefits packages for players were reworked, to the benefit of players, as well. Additional issues covered in the agreement of 1977 included team player limits, disciplinary authority of the Commissioner, and changes in the rules regarding trades. Finally, the agreement included a no-strike clause.

In 1982, after the 1977 agreement expired, the NFLPA called for a strike and players refused to play for two months from late September to late November. This walkout caused the cancellation of seven games for each of the teams. The resolve of the players led to hurried negotiations and a quick agreement to terms. The 1982 agreement, signed on November 17, brought the players back to the field to complete the now-shortened season. Under this agreement, a minimum salary for each player was set up based on experience and benefits packages were increased. The labor agreement also included a severance pay agreement, an issue that was not included in other sports' labor agreements at the time. This would serve as the last agreement until 1993.

The 1993 contract is the basis for the current bargaining agreement. Since 1993, the agreement has been extended twice: 1998 and 2002. The current collective bargaining agreement runs through 2007. This agreement, like those before it, increased the benefits packages of players, reaching a league-wide total of over $1 billion. These benefits applied to both current and retired players.

The 1993 agreement also included a significant new issue: team salary caps. The salary cap was introduced as a way to prevent player salaries from hurting the overall profitability of the game. The players received concessions in the area of free agency to balance the agreement. The salary cap limits overall team expenditures on player salaries by capping team payrolls at a certain percentage of league revenues. Players have been limited in recent years to a salary cap of about 63% of revenues. Players are guaranteed at least 56% of revenues as a league minimum, though. The salary cap is enforced through the commissioner's office, which must approve each contract in the league.

Current labor negotiations revolve around the scope of revenues to be included in the salary cap formula. While the players want to increase the forms of revenue that are counted toward the cap basis, the owners point to increasing infrastructure expenses as too costly to allow such an increase. However, since the current agreement lasts until 2007, both sides have plenty of time to come to an agreement. Both sides would like to remain a part of the only major professional sport to not have a work stoppage since 1982.

The UFL and UFL Owners

The United Football League (UFL) is a fictionalized football league that has been created for the purposes of this simulation. For all intents and purposes, the UFL's history, operating and collective bargaining procedures and agreements are essentially equivalent to those of the NFL.

The 40 teams that are currently part of the United Football League (UFL) are owned by entities ranging from single private owners to entire communities serving as owners. The UFL owners, coaches, and their representatives meet to vote and discuss issues that affect the management and rules employed by the league. The following are some examples of issues that have come up and been decided upon during these meetings:

- League Realignment
- Disciplinary actions for misconduct by players, coaches, and owners
- Instant Replay
- Rule changes regarding game play
- Revenue sharing issues
- TV and other licensing agreements

Owners deliberate the issues and vote on whether measures will be passed or postponed for further research and thought. Some issues are easily resolved among the owners but some are points of serious contention. Teams must negotiate with each other for what they hopefully believe is a platform that is in the best interest of the game. The UFL also meets to decide upon a concerted platform to serve as a starting point for negotiations with the UFLPA regarding labor. The owners and UFLPA have increased their level of cooperation over the years but, as in most cases, labor and management can have quite adversarial relationships.

UFLPA

The United Football League Players Association (UFLPA) represents the players in the UFL. The UFLPA is a union that represents the players on all teams and has been recognized since 1993. The players meet with representatives from the UFLPA to discuss issues that are important to them, and issues that they would like addressed. These issues are typically addressed when the owners and the UFLPA meet to negotiate a new or modified CBA. Several issues have been brought up by the players and the UFLPA in the past that are now included in the CBA. These issues include:

- Free agency
- Guaranteed percentage of gross revenues
- Product Endorsements
- Drug Testing

Since the creation of the UFLPA, the players have had much more organized input as to what issues are included in the CBA. The UFLPA gives the players one uniform body to speak for all of them. Furthermore, it gives the players much more leverage in negotiating with the owners. Negotiations with owners have improved over the years. However, there are still many issues that the sides disagree on. This relationship with the owners is an important one because the UFLPA and the owners must reach agreements that are best for both parties. Currently, there are several issues that need to be negotiated as the current CBA moves closer to expiration.

Summary of the Current Collective Bargaining Agreement[1]

Salary Cap

Summary of Current Agreement

Article XXIV states that the salary cap is set by a percentage of Defined Gross Revenues (DGR). DGR are composed of all revenues that are received by the UFL and all UFL teams in a given league year that primarily come from the performance of players in UFL football games.

Included in DGR are gate receipts and proceeds from radio and television contracts. Revenues excluded from the DGR that are not derived from the performance of UFL players include the proceeds from the sale or trade of player contracts, the sale of an UFL franchise, "revenue sharing" among UFL teams, interest income, and real estate and property sales. DGR includes allocated revenues from Personal Seat Licenses (PSLs) received by the UFL, any UFL team, affiliate, or third party. PSLs include all revenues gained through the right to acquire or retain tickets to UFL games. PSLs are not included in DGR when the proceeds are used to fund the renovation or construction of a new stadium. However, the revenues from PSLs will be allocated in prior years if the new stadium renovation or construction brings about an increase in team revenue. Up to $5 million per year can be deducted from DGR for payments made to the UFLPA. A credit of up to $8 million will be excluded from DGR for all contributions made to UFL charities by or on behalf of UFL Properties or UFL Films. Up to $25 million can be deducted from DGR for contributions to youth football programs.

Salary, as defined in this agreement, is the compensation in money, property, investments, loans, or anything else of value to which an UFL player is entitled, according to the terms of the contract, excluding benefits. Salary for a certain period includes all salary attributable to that specific time period.

If a player costs per UFL team equal or exceed 67% of the DGR for a given year, a salary cap and minimum salary standard are put in place for the next year.

Section 3 includes a rule that, if a salary cap is in effect, all players in the league are required to be paid a minimum of 58% of total DGR. If the player costs for all UFL Teams during a league year in which a salary cap is in place are less than 58% of the DGR, the UFL will pay an amount equal to the difference directly to players who played on UFL Teams during that season.

Section 4 ensures that salary caps have been negotiated for the following year and will be implemented as follows during seasons in which they are in effect:
> **2005**-65.5% of the Projected Defined Gross Revenues, less League-wide Projected Benefits, divided by the number of Teams playing in the UFL during the year.

The actual dollar amount of the Salary Cap cannot be less than the actual dollar amount of any Salary Cap in effect during the previous league year. If the total player costs of the UFL Teams during any league year (when a salary cap is in place) fall below 60% of DGR, the Salary Cap for the next league year will be increased. For every 1% that costs fall below 60% there will be a 1% increase in the Salary Cap. For example, if total player costs fall below 59% of actual DGR the Salary Cap will increase by 1% of projected DGR.

Reasonable security costs up to $250,000 can be deducted from the calculation of the salary cap for each team. The teams shall negotiate with the owners in good faith to determine the appropriate amount to deduct.

Cash salary includes a player's salary, bonus amounts, incentives, and anything else paid or given to the player during that league year that is valued (this includes the fair market value of automobiles gifted to players).

---

[1] The summary of the "Current Collective Bargaining Agreement" section contains excerpts and paraphrased excerpts from the NFL Collective Bargaining Agreement that is available at http://www.nflpa.org/CBA/CBA_Complete.aspx. Simulation participants are encouraged to review the full text of this agreement available online. All of the terms of the NFL CBA apply to the UFL CBA.

Section 5 reports that when a salary cap is enforced, there will be a minimum team Salary of 56% of the DGR (excluding league wide benefits) divided by the number of teams currently playing in the UFL. A team may pay in excess of the minimum team salary as long as the salary cap is not exceeded.

Issues to be Negotiated
A couple of salary cap issues may be subject to negotiations. They are as follows:

- **Salary Cap DGR Percentage:** The salary cap is the maximum that all players' salaries can total for any given team in the UFL. The UFLPA wants the salary cap as high as possible to ensure high player individual salaries. The owners, of course, would like to save as much money as they can. The Salary Cap is very important because it ensures competitiveness throughout the league in addition to a level playing field for all teams. Negotiations should focus on what percentage of the Projected Defined Gross Revenues will comprise a salary cap.

- **Minimum Team Salary:** The minimum team salary is the lowest possible amount that owners are required to pay players. This amount can be split among players in any way deemed appropriate by the each owner as long as the minimum salary is met for each player. The UFLPA wants the minimum team salary as high as possible. And, of course, owners, especially the less affluent ones, would like to set a lower minimum team salary. Negotiations here will deal with what percentage of the DGR will be set as the minimum team salary.

Player Benefits

Summary of Current Agreement
Article XLVI establishes the entirety of all player benefit costs. This includes benefits ranging from pension funds to workers' compensation and player scholarships. Section 1 outlines a cap on total costs for the player benefits. Section 2 outlines the UFLPA's right to restore any benefits cut from a player or group's benefits package for one year. Section 3 defines all player benefit costs in the CBA. Section 6 outlines the limitations on the owners' obligation to contribute to player benefit plans. Article XLVII outlines the specifics of the players' retirement plan. Section 3 of this section outlines the benefit credits for each adjusted time period from pre-1982 to the present. Section 6 of this article outlines the definition of disability for the purpose of compensation and disability benefits. Article XLVIII discusses the Second Career Savings Plan and the matching contributions to this savings plan made by the teams to each player's account. It also discusses the players' Annuity Plan and the eligibility requirements for this plan. Section 2 of this article covers contributions to this annuity and the minimum level of contributions required by each team. Section 3 of this article discusses eligibility requirements for the Second Career Savings Plan and the Annuity plan.

Issues to be Negotiated
Several player benefits issues may be subject to negotiations. They are as follows:

- **Amount of matching contribution for the Second Career Savings Plan:** The players want to maintain the current practices concerning matching, while the owners want to institute a plan more similar to those in general business environments. Under the current plan, the owners must contribute $2 for every dollar a player places in the Second Career Savings Plan.

- **Eligibility for player annuity program:** The UFLPA wants first year players to be fully vested in the player annuity plan from the first day of their contract while the owners would like to increase the waiting period to five years before they are required to match their players' investments. Another point of negotiation is whether or not the eligibility requirements should be modified, i.e. when the player can begin drawing on his annuity.

- **Insurance prescription drug co-pays:** The owners are trying to decrease their medical insurance costs. They want to double the medical insurance co-pay for medication from $5 for generic and $10 for name brand drugs to $10 and $20 respectively. The UFLPA is strongly opposed to any increase in medical costs for players.

- **Eligibility of players for severance pay:** Under the current agreement, players are eligible for severance pay only after they have accumulated 2 credited years in the league. The players feel that because of the hazardous nature of their profession, they face enough uncertainty without worrying about making it through two years of play without injury or incident.

Conduct

Summary of Current Agreement

Article VIII on Club discipline is very straightforward. Section 1 outlines the maximum fines that a player may incur for specific behavior. Section 2 states that all Clubs must publish and make available to all players at the beginning of pre-season training camp a complete list of the offenses and repercussions outlined in the previous section. Section 3 ensures that all players are treated equally, or uniformly, in regards to conduct expectations and penalties. The Club does have the right to specify particular events that may cause the discipline taken to be escalated; however, it must apply these new standards uniformly to all players. According to another article in the agreement, however, the Commissioner has the right to impose disciplinary action upon a player, which can be supplemented with or override any action taken by the Club for the same conduct. Section 5 sets a limit on the amount of money that can be withdrawn at one time from a player's check. According to the current agreement, no more than $1,000 can be deducted from a player's check per pay period. So, if a player was to collect $3,000 in fines, three of his pay periods would be subject to garnishment.

Issues to be Negotiated

Several conduct issues may be subject to negotiations. They are as follows:

- **Weight limit:** This refers to the maximum amount that a player may weigh at period weigh-ins. Players may view this as an issue that infringes on their personal rights, and that weight is irrelevant as long as they are still able to maintain their usual level of performance. On the other hand, owners feel that players must maintain certain weight in order to ensure physical stamina necessary for their particular position. Weight limit can be negotiated according to the amount and frequency of the fine, how many weigh-ins may be conducted, or what limit constitutes "over-weight."

- **Late reporting for or absence from pre-season training camp:** All players under contract must report to pre-season training camp and games that take place at the camp. "Late" is not taken to mean timeliness by a few minutes but a significant amount of time, such as one a day or more. Players may feel that this issue is unreasonable, since it is not a season activity. Owners will feel that the players are contracted for this activity, which is necessary for maintaining season performance standards. The definition of "late" may be clarified and the league year penalties may be adjusted to preserve uniformity.

- **Unexcused missed 1) mandatory off-season training camp, 2) team meeting, 3) practice, 4) curfew, 5) bed check, 6) appointment with Club physician or trainer, or 7) scheduled promotional activity:** This issue details a number of activities that are mandatory for players to attend. Players feel that some of these issues are excessively fined. Owners feel that the players' performance suffers when they do not show up to appointments that are important to the future performance of the team. Fine amounts and which absences are deemed finable can be negotiated.

- **Reporting of Injuries:** Players are expected to follow any programs or guidelines that the Club physician or trainer recommends for treatment of an injury. Additionally, it is the responsibility of the player to report any injuries to the Club physician or trainer. Players may feel that this is a privacy issue, and one that is subject to their personal discretion. They know their bodies or have their own physicians that know how to treat an injury. On the other hand, owners view this as a liability issue; if a player is hurt, his condition may worsen and the Club's performance may be subject to repercussions from his absence. They feel that their medical staff should prescribe rehabilitation programs and that these mandated programs must be strictly followed. A specific time period and/or severity ranking may be negotiated in addition to the amount of the fine, if any.

- **Loss of playbook or game plan:** This issue addresses a player's responsibility to keep team strategy confidential. While a player might not intentionally leave a playbook or game plan in a public place, his doing so might jeopardize the team's competitive positioning. Players see this as an accidental mistake that should be easily forgiven, but owners view this as a violation of confidentiality. The inclusion of this issue as a conduct violation may be discussed, as well as any extenuating circumstances and the proposed amount of the penalty.

- **Ejection from game:** Players may be ejected from an UFL game if they exhibit behavior that is deemed excessively inappropriate by the game officials. Owners believe that they should have the right to fine players for this type of activity in order to help maintain their Club's image and performance level. Players believe that a mandated fine would not allow extenuating circumstances to be taken into account. Negotiations on this issue are based on the mandatory nature of the fine and the fine amount.

- **Maximum deduction of fines from paycheck:** This issue refers to the amount of fines that may be deducted from a player's check each pay period. Some players may see this issue as unfair, especially if their check is not as much as another player's. Owners will see this issue as an extension of the "uniformity" that they try to bestow upon all players. The amount of the maximum deduction should be discussed. Also, instead of a fixed amount, a percentage deduction from the pay check may be negotiated.

Likeness and Public Appearance

Summary of Current Agreement
In Article V, Section 4 of the current agreement, players cede some of the control over their public appearance to the owners of their respective clubs. Certain rights are still left with the players, though. The agreement specifies that any use of six or more players for a promotional purpose constitutes a group to be considered under the Group Licensing Program that is run by the UFLPA. The agreement is broad enough to cover any use of the player or his likeness. Signature, name, voice, photographs, and biographical information are all included as likeness uses. Usage restrictions extend to all kinds of products: games, clothing, trading cards, etc.

Article VII, Section 2 also describes the rights of Clubs in determining the appearance of players both on the field and in situations where the Club is being represented. The language in the current agreement is vague and allows for interpretation. The agreement does prohibit Clubs from regulating hair style (including facial hair).

Article LV, Section 1 states that Slubs cannot unreasonably refuse to allow a player to endorse any product of his choosing.

In Section 3, the UFL and none of the Clubs currently have a rule prohibiting or limiting the type of footwear or gloves chosen by players for use on the field. An exception to this would be any rules or limitations agreed to by the UFLPA.

Section 4 provides that players cannot be unreasonably required by their Club to appear on radio or television

Section 6 presents the overall view that critical statements made by UFL Players about their own team, another team, an UFL coach, the operations and policies of their team, and other aspects of the game are frowned upon by UFL and the Management Council. These offenses cause damage to the UFL's reputation and the player's team, and therefore the current agreement states that "best efforts" will be taken to control critical comments made in public.

Issues to be Negotiated
Several likeness and public appearance issues may be subject to negotiations. They are as follows:

- **Definition of "reasonable" regarding player appearance:** A specific definition of "reasonable" is not found in the current agreement. This lack of specificity could lead to disagreements between players and Clubs in the future. Players wish to dress in their preferred attire that reflects their own style. Owners feel that control is important in this area because the players are acting as representatives for the Clubs and can have a dramatic effect on public perception of the game. Negotiations in this area should focus on any specific lines that can be drawn regarding "reasonable" control by the owners.

- **Definition of "representing the Clubs":** The restrictions agreed to in the above section apply only to situations where the player is representing the Club in some fashion. Owners would like to make scope of representation as broad as possible to prevent any player from embarrassing the club, i.e. when out at dinner, clubs or bars, etc. Players would like the idea of representation to apply only to official Club-sponsored activities to maintain their rights.

- **Product Endorsements:** Should players be allowed to endorse any product that they choose, even if it is not in the best interest of his team or the league? From a player's perspective, the right to endorse products is very important because of the lucrative nature of these ventures. The Club identifies some types of products as inappropriate and unacceptable for its players to promote. Players would like to avoid restrictions if possible, but owners are interested in establishing criteria of products that they feel are inappropriate for their players to endorse. Should owners have a right to prohibit players from endorsing certain products?

- **Attire:** As the exposure and popularity of individual players has risen, their desire for individuality and self-expression has increased concurrently. Players would like to have the ability to express their individuality by wearing various colors, brands, and accessories such as jewelry and headgear. Players also fear that any attire restrictions could interfere with their own apparel contracts and possibly cause the loss of lucrative endorsements in the future. However, owners feel it is the best interest of themselves and the Club's image to have some control over the level of self-expression that players have. Owners also stand to benefit from any specific product restrictions, especially particular brands, because advertisers may have to provide more team-wide endorsement contracts that would improve the profitability of their Club. Thus, acceptable items of attire and any restrictions are negotiable.

- **Definition of "Unreasonably":** According to the agreement, Clubs may not "unreasonably" require their players to appear in certain media spots, advertisements, or interviews. Topics to be negotiated as reasonable/unreasonable include:
  - Time periods: how soon before/after a game or event is unreasonable?
  - Days of the week: are there certain days of the week that players would not like to be on duty?
  - Holidays: what holidays are considered to be unreasonable for appearances?
  - In-season/Off-season: do players consider off-season requirements to be unreasonable, or do they feel the in-season is an even less appropriate time?

  Players would like to have some control over when they are required to make appearances and to have specified definitions to delineate reasonable from unreasonable required appearances. Owners would like to have as much access to their players as possible, allowing them to require appearances whenever it is most beneficial to the Club and its profitability. Thus, the owners like the current general terminology.

- **"Criticism" and Subsequent Penalties:** It is necessary to define what exactly makes a comment "criticism". Players are passionate about their sport, and may say things that are inappropriate when they are being interviewed by the press. They would like to have as much freedom of expression as possible, while the owners would like to keep any negative comments or bad press under control. If a player makes a public comment that is deemed inappropriate, what sort of punishment will he face? The owners' main goal in penalizing players is to ensure that the "criticism" will be curtailed, but players desire to not have severe penalties for critical comments made in public. Penalties, if any, can be monetary or involve suspension or community service, and can be issued at different levels, depending on the severity of the comment, if so desired.

Drug Testing

Summary of Current Agreement
Article XLIV states that the League may conduct random drug tests for steroids with limits to the number of test decided upon by the Commissioner and the UFLPA. The number of allowable tests is not disclosed and will be a point of debate for students. Section 5 covers substance abuse for UFL players.

Issues to be Negotiated
Several drug testing issues may be subject to negotiations. They are as follows:

- **Random testing**
  - **Advanced notice:** This will refer to what kind of notice, if any, must be given to players before they are required take a drug test. This will also cover what kind of contact a player must maintain with the league office so that they will be available for a test and how long a player has to respond and take the test before they are considered late. Players consider this important because they currently must maintain strict contact with league offices and feel this encroaches upon their free time. Owners feel that players must make themselves available for testing at any place and anytime. How much, if any, advance notice should a player be given before a drug test is conducted?

  - **Number of tests per year:** This refers to the number of times in a calendar year that a player may be tested for drugs and/or banned substances. Players view this as important because they believe that excessive testing is a violation of rights. Owners, however, have a strong interest in maintaining the integrity of the game. This can range from 0 (no substance tests) to any number that can be agreed upon. Note that considerations such as minimum times between tests can also be discussed in this area.

- **How banned substances will be determined:** This will designate who will determine whether a substance should be considered banned by the UFL. Players view this as important because substances they currently use or substance that are readily available over the counter may suddenly show up on the banned substance list. Several players claim they had no idea they were taking banned substances or contained amounts of banned substances. Owners again do not want players to gain advantage by taking supplements that the UFL has not studied and deemed acceptable. Both sides would like to resolve how a substance is classified as "banned."

- **Non-random testing plans:** This refers to fixed dates during the season and off-season at which players will be subject to comprehensive drug tests. This again is important to the players because they believe that excessive testing is a violation of rights, while owners have an interest in maintaining the integrity of the game. Note that these tests, though, are not as important to players as the random tests are, because they know exactly when these tests will occur. Owners may find this more important because the players will typically be heading into training camp or the season when these tests are administered. This can range from 0 (no substance tests) to any number that can be agreed upon.

- **Non-positive test violations:** This refers to any activity that a player engages in that facilitates the use of a banned substance by another player. This will include providing banned substances to others or referring other players to individuals that provide banned substances. Owners feel that a player who promotes or provides banned substances to other players may cause even more damage than those who use them. Players find this important because they may find themselves liable for providing a substance that they did not know were illegal or introducing friends to other friends. The types of behavior and possible punishments related to activities that allow for the proliferation of drug and substance abuse in the UFL are the subjects of this negotiation point.

General Rules

Rule #1
- Individual team members may not discuss any part of the simulation including research, ideas, plans, strategies, or positions with members of the opposing team at any time during the negotiation. Teams as a whole are also restricted from discussing any information, strategies, or positions with other teams. This rule applies to any information sharing that is not administered or allowed by the instructor (commissioner) of the simulation.

Rule #2
- All students are encouraged to use creativity and imaginative thinking in preparing their strategies and plans. Ideas that do not rationally and plausibly follow the background information provided or the current Collective Bargaining Agreement will not be allowed for submission. Teams are encouraged to actively seek creative solutions that logically follow the information provided in the instructions and background information. All questionable strategies and ideas will be ruled upon by the instructor (commissioner).

Rule #3
- The ground rules that are established by each team should be followed as if they are general rules of the negotiation. Failure to follow these or any other rules will be dealt with by each team individually as well as by the instructor of the game.

Rule #4
- Teams may conduct additional research for information to support their arguments and issues. Any research findings used in the negotiations must reasonably apply to the situation(s) and not alter the issues and facts in this simulation.

Rule #5
- The instructor (commissioner) will determine negotiation and assignment deadlines. Deadlines will not be extended unless there are extraordinary circumstances affecting the completion of the deliverables.

Good Luck!

Format

The instructor will play the role of the UFL Commissioner and determine the format of this exercise.

Negotiation Roles

This exercise calls for five students to be placed on the UFL owners' team and five students to be placed on the UFLPA's team. Fewer students can use this exercise; however, some students may be forced to take on more than one role for each of the teams. There will be one student elected from the UFLPA's and the owners' team that will act as the teams head representative in the negotiation process. Each of the five team members on both sides will be a representative in charge of the following issues:

- ☐ Salary Cap
- ☐ Player Benefits
- ☐ Conduct
- ☐ Likeness
- ☐ Drug Policy

Each of these students will be given the task of shaping the platform and policies in these categories for their respective teams to take on those issues.

Meeting Schedule

Round 1
The first round of meetings will consist of an intra-team and inter-team meeting that should each last 30 minutes. Both teams will decide amongst themselves how they want to manage the negotiation as a team. A team representative will be elected, and all members will provide a signed document to the commissioner that outlines the *tentative ground rules* that were reached during the intra-team meetings. The inter-group meeting will allow both teams to come to a consensus as to the *tentative ground rules* of the negotiations between the two teams. This agreement will be supervised by the UFL commissioner and must be signed by both Owner and UFLPA representatives.

Round 2
This round will consist of independent meetings amongst each of the two teams and should last one hour. Each team will review the current CBA and create a plan of action for their negotiation. Each team will have a document that details the current CBA terms and will decide how they will be prioritized.

Round 3
This round will consist of two separate independent meetings between the two teams and should last 1 hour each. One of these meetings will revolve around non-economic issues and the other meeting will focus on economic issues. All members of each team will be required to attend these meetings. Each team will assign values for each issue and will enter them onto the sheets provided. These numeric priorities will be the basis each side's negotiations. The document produced during these meetings will be signed by the appropriate representatives.

Round 4
This round will involve five separate one-on-one meetings that should last 1 hour each. The representatives for each particular issue will meet and discuss their issue with the other team's representative on that particular issue. Both representatives will come to an agreement on their issues and sign a document that outlines their results. These results will be used as a starting point in the final negotiation.

Round 5
This intra-team meeting will allow each representative from each team to debrief the results of Round 4's negotiation. The debriefing should last 1 hour. The groups will fill out a form that explains the results of the prior negotiation and where they want the negotiation to go in the final round. This form will be used as the negotiation template for the final round.

Round 6
The final negotiation will be attended by all students and will last 1 to 1 ½ hours. The team representative for each side will manage the negotiation and be the spokesman for their respective team. This negotiation should follow the same

format as Round 4. The final agreement will be signed by the UFL commissioner and the head representative from each team. This document will detail the final agreement.

Meeting 1A – UFLPA Formation Meeting

Meeting 1B – Owner Formation Meeting

Meeting 1C – Negotiation Formation Meeting

Meeting 2A – UFLPA reviews current CBA terms

Meeting 2B – Owners review current CBA terms

Meeting 3A – UFLPA non-economic strategy discussion and formation

Meeting 3B – UFLPA economic strategy discussion and formation

Meeting 3C – Owners non-economic strategy discussion and formation

Meeting 3D – Owners economic strategy discussion and formation

Meeting 4A – Owners and UFLPA salary cap negotiations

Meeting 4B – Owners and UFLPA benefits negotiation

Meeting 4C – Owners and UFLPA conduct negotiation

Meeting 4D – Owners and UFLPA likeness negotiation

Meeting 4E – Owners and UFLPA drug policy negotiation

Meeting 5A – UFLPA debriefing

Meeting 5B – Owners debriefing

Meeting 6 – Final Negotiation between UFLPA and Owners

Meeting Schedule

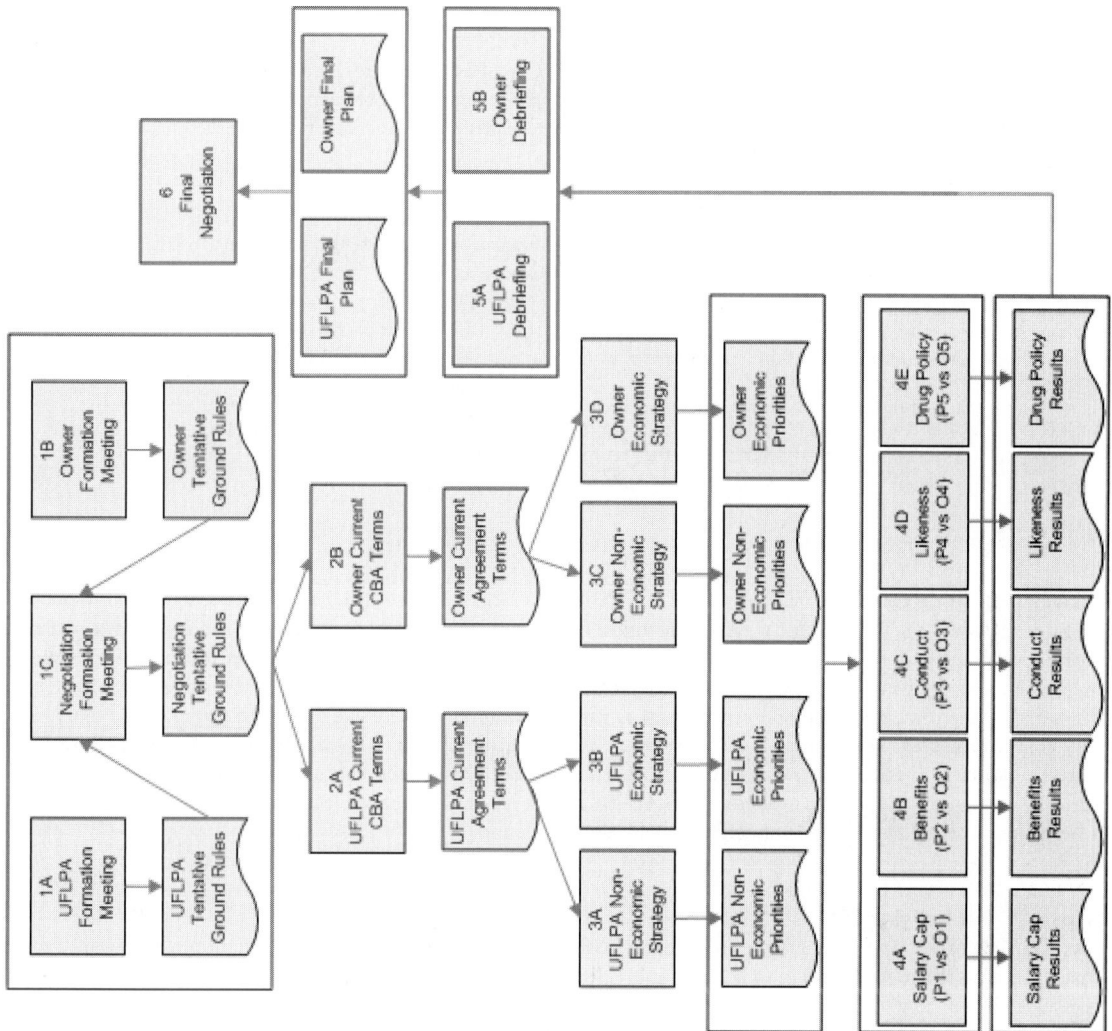

Negotiation Roles

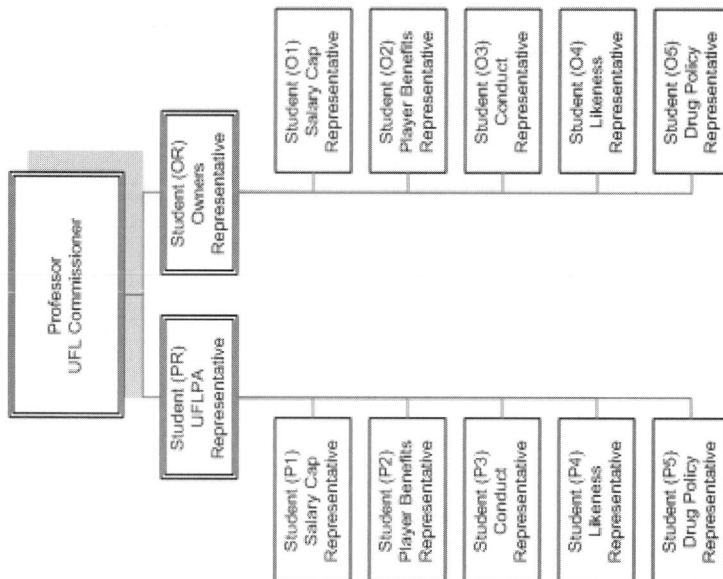

Legend

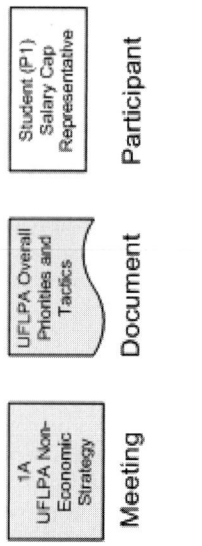

15

Supplemental Negotiation Spreadsheet

Along with the text materials in this negotiation simulation, you have been provided with a supplemental spreadsheet application, which should provide better understanding of the interactions between the different factors that affect the UFL salary cap. Your instructor will inform you of the spreadsheet's specific use within the negotiation. However, you are welcome, and encouraged, to examine the tool independently as a means of furthering your understanding of the complex salary cap issue.

To use the spreadsheet application, open it and read the information found on the welcome screen. This will provide you with some basic information about the application's purpose and usage. Next, follow the instructions to add your team's name to the worksheet. You will then see the main screen, which contains several inputs, that you are able to change, affecting the team salary cap. For more information on the specific factors that affect the salary cap and how to adjust them, please select the "Help" option from either the main screen or the input screen.

Negotiation Roles

Players

Player 1: T-Bone Carver

T-Bone Carver is a star player for what has historically been one of the league's top teams. He is known equally for his attitude as much as for his athletic abilities. Throughout T-Bone's career, he has cared more about himself than the team; he views the game as a way to make money and nothing more. T-Bone believes that his salary would be much higher if his team wasn't already pushing the salary cap, and would therefore like to see the cap raised as much as possible. He also has several lucrative endorsement deals and doesn't want any negotiated agreement to lessen his earning capacity. Finally, T-Bone has a history of criticizing both his team's staff and his teammates. Instead of thinking that this behavior is a counterproductive, he feels it "lights a fire under" the subjects of his comments. He, therefore, doesn't want to see restrictions or penalties on speaking his mind.

Player 2: Uri Kchylnzzm

Uri Kchylnzzm is a place kicker for a small market UFL team. While his kicking stats have not been stellar, Uri has managed to perform well enough to keep his job. He has not, however, moved beyond the league minimum salary. Because of this, he would like to see the league minimum increased to bring his salary closer to that of the 'stars' on his team. An increase in pay would also help Uri by lowering the impact of his many fines on his earnings. His hot temper has gotten him into arguments with referees, opposing players, and even team staff. He would like to keep the maximum fine deduction for pay periods low so that he can support his eight children. Uri loves his children and his family, and wants to be with them (and not at team functions) as much as possible. In the past, Uri had an altercation with T-Bone Carver. Uri believes that some of T-Bone's critical comments have closed off opportunities to advance his career.

Player 3: Sandy Boss

Sandy Boss is a star player on a mid-market team. He has had discipline problems, both on the field and off. He would like to see management have less control over what happens on the field, limiting fines for 'inappropriate' behavior. Sandy would also like to see team management with no control over his actions when he is not actually playing or practicing. He believes that his private life is his own. His team's management is concerned after an incident where Sandy was found in the company of a minor during the off-season. Sandy's other major concern is the drug testing policy. He is currently using anabolic steroids and other substances but has found a way to avoid being detected by current policies. He would like to make sure that no new policies are enacted.

Player 4: Bruce Sandler

Bruce Sandler is a player near the end of a long and successful career. While not headed for the Hall of Fame, Bruce is widely regarded as an excellent offensive lineman. His primary concern with the new agreement is to make sure that retirement benefits are as high as possible. Even though he has been successful over his career, Bruce has never made the high dollar figures that the sport's superstars make. Bruce also feels like his team's doctors and trainers are too much in control of his body. He thinks that, after 4 knee surgeries, he is very capable of determining when he needs to rehab and when he doesn't. Bruce is also annoyed at the complaints of his coach for his arrival at camp overweight. Bruce feels like the added weight makes him harder to get past, and would like to lower or remove penalties for this infraction.

Player 5: Kenneth Drake

Kenneth Drake is a rookie who was not selected during the draft. He was signed as a free agent by a powerful team in the league. However, the starter at his position is entrenched and has been to several pro bowls. Ken is therefore not able to command a very high salary. He would like to see the minimum salary (which is his salary) raised as much as possible. Because of his low salary, Ken is not enthused about attending all the practices and team meetings. He would like these penalties, which are costing him a lot, to be reduced or removed in the new agreement. Ken's ultimate goal is to play enough years to be vested in retirement annuities and get out of the league—provided he doesn't become a superstar. He currently has an offer from a hometown car dealership that would supplement a retirement payment.

Owners

Owner 1: George Stenton

George is the owner of a large market team that competes near the top of its division every year. He advocates raising the salary cap because he wants to field the most competitive team possible, something he feels his fans deserve. George believes, though, that the team should share in more of the licensing and product endorsement revenues since the team is responsible for much of the player's popularity in his view. George's other primary concern with this negotiation is his insistence that players be held accountable for not reporting injuries or following team rehab plans. He believes that his investment in the players gives them a duty to follow the team's regulations. George has a very spiteful relationship with Leroy Smithson, who disagrees with George on almost every issue related to the economics of the game. He also harbors resentment for Pat Carlson because his team manages to consistently beat Mr. Stenton's team.

Owner 2: Leroy Smithson

Leroy is the spokesman for a community owned small market team. He is looking to push for a lower salary cap to help increase his team's competitiveness. Current conditions are making it difficult for the team to make a profit. He is also looking for any opportunity possible to increase his team's visibility through promotional activities. Leroy would also like to negotiate terms that would make his players less likely to criticize his team in public. He currently has to cope with players complaining to the press that the facilities are out of date and the owners' commitment to winning is too low. Leroy has little respect for George Stenton, because Leroy feels that George tries to "buy" his success rather than earn it.

Owner 3: Lee Fairson

Lee is the owner of a mid-market team that is beloved by its fans. One of the most important issues to Lee is that his team's image stays positive. He supports issues that keep players from projecting a negative image, including restrictions on activities both on the field and off, stronger drug tests, and restrictions on the products that players can endorse. Mr. Fairson is interested in the integrity of the game and the value delivered to his fans. He comes from a blue collar family, a family much like many of his fans. Lee is a forgiving man, but he still harbors some ill will toward Phil Nixon because of some questionable practices employed by Nixon to attain of Fairson's former players.

Owner 4: Pat Carlson

Pat is the owner of a club that finishes near the top of the league each year. He is just as rabid of a fan as his Club's most ardent supporters. Pat has a "win at all costs" attitude that occasionally causes friction between him and some of the other owners. Pat supports increasing fines for players who do anything that might jeopardize his chances to win, including late reporting, being overweight, and failure to report injury. However, since Pat's team lost the Super Bowl three years ago due to a playbook that fell into the wrong hands (at least that's Pat's explanation of why his team lost), Pat has been very supportive of stiff penalties for a loss of playbook. Pat admires what Lee Fairson has done with his organization, and the two have neighboring condos in the Rocky Mountains.

Owner 5: Phil Nixon

Phil is the owner of a mid-market team in a rebuilding phase. His team consists of several big names that he has recently signed and a large group of rookies he believes will be stars. Phil would like to see the salary cap rise because he'd like to sign a few more star veterans in order to hasten his team's return to the top. Phil believes in discipline to build team unity, and supports harsh penalties for players who get out of line. He is also concerned, due to his team's makeup, with how soon players are eligible for retirement annuities and severance pay issues. Phil has been known to stretch the rules to get what he wants, including "stealing" some of Lee Fairson's star players.

Negotiation Forms

The following pages contain the forms for use in the individual negotiations and group meetings.

Meeting 1A: Formation Meeting
Goal: Establish Intra-team and Inter-group Ground Rules

Instructions: *Intra-team meeting (30 minutes):* Team members should meet and discuss basic rules that will govern the entire negotiation. These rules are meant to establish structure, team responsibility, and disciplinary actions among UFLPA members. The contract should name the elected UFLPA representative who will represent the group in all decisions. All team members must sign the contract.

Inter-group meeting (30 minutes): Team members should meet and discuss tentative rules that will govern the entire negotiation. These rules are meant to establish the way in which decisions will be made between the UFLPA and UFL owners; time limits, behavioral limitations, and penalties for non-agreements are examples of issues to be included in the overall contract.

UFLPA Agreement

Union Members: _____   Date: _____
                _____
                _____
                _____

Meeting 1A Continued

<u>**UFLPA Proposed Ground Rules for Inter-group Negotiation Governance**</u>

Meeting 1B: Owner Formation Meeting

Goal: Establish Intra-team and Inter-group Ground Rules

Instructions: *Intra-team meeting (30 minutes):* Team members should meet and discuss basic rules that will govern the entire negotiation. These rules are meant to establish structure, team responsibility, and disciplinary actions among UFL owners. The contract should name the elected UFL owner representative who will represent the group in all decisions. All team members must sign the contract.

Inter-group meeting (30 minutes): Team members should meet and discuss tentative rules that will govern the entire negotiation. These rules are meant to establish the way in which decisions will be made between the UFLPA and UFL owners; time limits, behavioral limitations, and penalties for non-agreements are examples of issues to be included in the overall contract.

UFL Owner Agreement

Owners: _____   Date: _____
        _____
        _____
        _____
        _____

UFL Owner Proposed Ground Rules for Inter-group Negotiation Governance

Meeting 1C: Negotiation Formation Meeting
Goal: Finalize Inter-group Ground Rules

Instructions: *Inter-group meeting (30 minutes):* Both groups should meet to discuss final ground rules. These rules are meant to establish the way in which decisions will be made between the UFLPA and UFL owners; time limits, behavioral limitations, and penalties for non-agreements are examples of issues to be included in the overall contract. Three signatures are required on this document: the owner representative, UFLPA representative, and the commissioner. Once signed, this contract is binding and violations will be prosecuted by the commissioner's office.

Ground Rules for Inter-group Negotiation Governance

UFLPA Representative: _____   Date: _____
Owner Representative: _____   Date: _____
Commissioner: _____   Date: _____

Meeting 2A: Current CBA Agreement
Goal: Understand the Current UFL Collective Bargaining Agreement

Instructions: *(1 hour)* The UFLPA should meet and discuss the current collective bargaining agreement terms. Team members should fill in the chart below with current agreement terms, and begin discussion of priorities and negotiation tactics.

Issue	Current Agreement Terms
Salary Cap	
Product Endorsements	
Advance Notice of Testing	
Number of Tests per Year	
Maximum Fines per Pay Period	
Banned Substances Determination	
Unexcused Absences	
Definition of Representing Clubs	
Definition of Unreasonably	
Attire	
Player's Appearance	
Weight Limit	
Minimum Team Salary	
Matching Contribution	
Criticism / Penalties	
Non-random Drug Testing	
Reporting of Injuries	
Ejection from Game	
Late Reporting	
Eligibility for Annuity	
Non-positive Drug Violations	
Loss of Playbook	
Eligibility for Severance Pay	
Drug Co-pay	

Meeting 2B: Current CBA Agreement

Goal: Understand the Current UFL Collective Bargaining Agreement

Instructions: *(1 hour)* The UFL owners should meet and discuss the current collective bargaining agreement terms. Team members should fill in the chart below with current agreement terms, and begin discussion of priorities and negotiation tactics.

Issue	Current Agreement Terms
Salary Cap	
Number of Tests per Year	
Definition of Representing Clubs	
Reporting of Injuries	
Unexcused Absences	
Weight Limit	
Criticism / Penalties	
Loss of Playbook	
Minimum Team Salary	
Matching Contribution	
Late Reporting	
Product Endorsements	
Advance Notice of Testing	
Non-random Drug Testing	
Definition of Unreasonably	
Banned Substances Determination	
Attire	
Ejection from Game	
Non-positive Drug Violations	
Eligibility for Annuity	
Player's Appearance	
Eligibility for Severance Pay	
Maximum Fine per Pay Period	
Drug Co-pay	

Meeting 3A: UFLPA Non-Economic Issues
Goal: Rank and Assign Point Values for the Non-economic Points of Negotiation

Instructions: *(1 hour)* In this meeting, your group should determine the point values for the issues listed below. Think carefully about how you distribute your points as your team will be judged by how well it meets its negotiation goals. Your team must assign a point value for each issue, choosing an amount between the minimum and maximum value determined by the issue's priority group.

Point values for the three priority levels may be distributed as follows (keep in mind that you only have 1000 total points and that some points in each category must carry over to the economic issues):

High: 550 total points; 40 points minimum per issue
Moderate: 300 total points; 20 points minimum per issue
Low: 150 total points; 10 points minimum per issue

Issue	Priority	Points
Product Endorsements	High	
Advance Notice of Testing	High	
Number of Tests per Year	High	
Maximum Fine per Pay Period	High	
Banned Substances Determination	High	
Unexcused Absences	High	
Definition of Representing Clubs	High	
Definition of Unreasonably	Moderate	
Attire	Moderate	
Player's Appearance	Moderate	
Weight Limit	Moderate	
Criticism / Penalties	Moderate	
Non-random Drug Testing	Moderate	
Reporting of Injuries	Low	
Ejection from Game	Low	
Late Reporting	Low	
Non-positive Drug Violations	Low	
Loss of Playbook	Low	

UFLPA Conduct Representative: _____ Date: _____
UFLPA Likeness Representative: _____ Date: _____
UFLPA Drug Policy Representative: _____ Date: _____

Meeting 3B: UFLPA Economic Issues
Goal: Rank and Assign Point Values for the Economic Points of Negotiation

Instructions: *(1 hour)* In this meeting, your group should determine the point values for the issues listed below. Think carefully about how you distribute your points as your team will be judged by how well it meets its negotiation goals. Your team must assign a point value for each issue, choosing an amount between the minimum and maximum value determined by the issue's priority group.

Point values for the three priority levels may be distributed as follows (keep in mind that you only have 1000 total points, including points, with priority-based limitations as specified below, assigned to non-economic issues):

High: 550 total points; 40 points minimum per issue
Moderate: 300 total points; 20 points minimum per issue
Low: 150 total points; 10 points minimum per issue

Issue	Priority	Points
Salary Cap	High	
Minimum Team Salary	Moderate	
Matching Contribution	Moderate	
Eligibility For Annuity	Low	
Eligibility For Severance Pay	Low	
Drug Co-pay	Low	

UFLPA Salary Cap Representative: _____ Date: _____
UFLPA Benefits Representative: _____ Date: _____

Meeting 3C: UFL Owners Non-Economic Issues
Goal: Rank and Assign Point Values for the Non-economic Points of Negotiation

Instructions: *(1 hour)* In this meeting, your group should determine the point values for the issues listed below. Think carefully about how you distribute your points as your team will be judged by how well it meets its negotiation goals. Your team must assign a point value for each issue, choosing an amount between the minimum and maximum value determined by the issue's priority group.

Point values for the three priority levels may be distributed as follows (keep in mind that you only have 1000 total points and that some points in each category must carry over to the economic issues):

High: 550 total points; 40 points minimum per issue
Moderate: 300 total points; 20 points minimum per issue
Low: 150 total points; 10 points minimum per issue

Issue	Priority	Points
Number of Tests Per Year	High	
Definition of Representing Clubs	High	
Reporting of Injuries	High	
Unexcused Absences	High	
Weight Limit	High	
Criticism / Penalties	High	
Loss of Playbook	High	
Late Reporting	Moderate	
Product Endorsements	Moderate	
Advance Notice of Testing	Moderate	
Non-random Drug Testing	Moderate	
Definition of Unreasonably	Moderate	
Banned Substances Determination	Moderate	
Attire	Low	
Ejection from Game	Low	
Non-positive Drug Violations	Low	
Player's Appearance	Low	
Maximum Fine per Pay Period	Low	

UFL Owners Conduct Representative: _____ Date: _____
UFL Owners Likeness Representative: _____ Date: _____
UFL Owners Drug Policy Representative: _____ Date: _____

Meeting 3D: UFL Owners Economic Issues
Goal: Rank and Assign Point Values for the Economic Points of Negotiation

Instructions: *(1 hour)* In this meeting, your group should determine the point values for the issues listed below. Think carefully about how you distribute your points as your team will be judged by how well it meets its negotiation goals. Your team must assign a point value for each issue, choosing an amount between the minimum and maximum value determined by the issue's priority group.

Point values for the three priority levels may be distributed as follows (keep in mind that you only have 1000 total points, including points, with priority-based limitations as specified below, assigned to non-economic issues):

High: 550 total points; 40 points minimum per issue
Moderate: 300 total points; 20 points minimum per issue
Low: 150 total points; 10 points minimum per issue

Issue	Priority	Points
Salary Cap	High	
Minimum Team Salary	Moderate	
Matching Contribution	Moderate	
Eligibility For Annuity	Low	
Eligibility For Severance Pay	Low	
Drug Co-pay	Low	

UFL Owners Salary Cap Representative: _____   Date: _____
UFL Owners Benefits Representative: _____   Date: _____

Meeting 4A: Salary Cap Results
Goal: Determine Final Settlements for Salary Cap

Instructions: *(30 minutes):* The UFLPA Salary Cap Representative and the UFL Owner Salary Cap representative will meet and discuss the issues below. The two representatives must agree on a final settlement for each issue and sign the contract.

<u>Issues</u>   <u>Results</u>

- Salary Cap DGR Percentage

- Minimum Team Salary

UFLPA Salary Cap Representative: _____   Date: _____
UFL Owner Salary Cap Representative: _____   Date: _____

Meeting 4B: Benefits Meeting
Goal: Determine Final Settlements for Benefits

Instructions: *(1 hour):* The UFLPA Benefits Representative and the UFL Owner Benefits Representative will meet and discuss the issues below. The two representatives must agree on a final settlement for each issue and sign the contract.

<u>**Issues**</u>   <u>**Results**</u>

- Amount of Matching Contribution

- Eligibility for Player Annuity

- Drug Co-pays

- Eligibility for Severance Pay

UFLPA Benefits Representative: _____ Date: _____
UFL Owner Benefits Representative: _____ Date: _____

Meeting 4C: Conduct Meeting
Goal: Determine Final Settlements for Conduct

Instructions: *(1 hour):* The UFLPA Conduct Representative and the UFL Owner Conduct Representative will meet and discuss the issues below. The two representatives must agree on a final settlement for each issue and sign the contract.

<u>**Issues**</u>   <u>**Results**</u>

- Weight Limit

- Reporting of Injuries

- Late Reporting

- Unexcused Absence

- Loss of Playbook

- Ejection from Game

- Maximum Fine per Pay Period

UFLPA Conduct Representative : _____   Date: _____
UFL Owner Conduct Representative: _____   Date: _____

Meeting 4D: Likeness Meeting
Goal: Determine Final Settlements for Likeness

Instructions: *(1 hour):* The UFLPA Likeness Representative and the UFL Owner Likeness Representative will meet and discuss the issues below. The two representatives must agree on a final settlement for each issue and sign the contract.

Issues	Results

- Definition of "Unreasonably"

- Definition of "Representing Clubs"

- Player's Appearance

- Product Endorsements

- Attire

- Criticism / Penalties

UFLPA Likeness Representative: _____ Date: _____
UFL Owner Likeness Representative: _____ Date: _____

Meeting 4E: Drug Policy Meeting

Goal: Determine Final Settlements for Drug Policy

Instructions: *(1 hour):* The UFLPA Drug Policy Representative and the UFL Owner Drug Policy representative will meet and discuss the issues below. The two representatives must agree on a final settlement for each issue and sign the contract.

Issues	Results

- Advance Notice of Testing

- Number of Tests per Year

- Banned Substances Determination

- Non-random Drug Testing

- Non-positive Drug Violations

UFLPA Drug Policy Representative: _____   Date: _____

UFL Owner Drug Policy Representative: _____   Date: _____

Meeting 5A: UFLPA Debriefing
Goal: Develop Strategy for Final Negotiation

Instructions: *(1 hour)* After your representatives have met with UFL owner representatives about your respective issues, your team must now report the outcomes of their meetings, explain why they are satisfied / dissatisfied with the outcome, and where the negotiation will go next. In the determination of the next steps, the team must decide whether or not they are flexible on an issue and finalize what the hopeful outcome will be.

Issue	Current Decision from Meeting 4	Reason for Satisfaction/ Dissatisfaction	Plan (Flexible/ Non-Flexible)	Hopeful Outcomes
Salary Cap				
Salary Cap DGR Percentage				
Minimum Team Salary				
Benefits				
Matching Contribution				
Eligibility for Annuity				
Drug Co-pay				
Eligibility for Severance Pay				
Conduct				
Weight Limit				
Reporting of Injuries				
Late Reporting				
Unexcused Absences				
Loss of Playbook				
Ejection from Game				
Maximum Fine per Pay Period				

Likeness

Definition of "Unreasonably"		
Definition of "Representing Clubs"		
Player's Appearance		
Product Endorsements		
Attire		
Criticism / Penalties		

Drug Testing

Advance Notice of Testing		
Number of Tests per Year		
Banned Substances Determination		
Non-random Drug Plan		
Non-positive Drug Violations		

Meeting 5B: UFL Owner Debriefing

Goal: Develop Strategy for Final Negotiation

Instructions: *(1 hour)* After your representatives have met with UFLPA representatives about your respective issues, your team must now report the outcomes of their meetings, explain why they are satisfied / dissatisfied with the outcome, and where the negotiation will go next. In the determination of the next steps, the team must decide whether or not they are flexible on an issue and finalize what the hopeful outcome will be.

Issue	Current Decision from Meeting 4	Reason for Satisfaction/ Dissatisfaction	Plan (Flexible/ Non-Flexible)	Hopeful Outcomes
Salary Cap				
Salary Cap DGR Percentage				
Minimum Team Salary				
Benefits				
Matching Contribution				
Eligibility for Annuity				
Drug Co-pay				
Eligibility for Severance Pay				
Conduct				
Weight Limit				
Reporting of Injuries				
Late Reporting				
Unexcused Absences				
Loss of Playbook				
Ejection from Game				
Maximum Fine per Pay Period				

Likeness

Definition of "Unreasonably"				
Definition of "Representing Clubs"				
Player's Appearance				
Product Endorsements				
Attire				
Criticism / Penalties				

Drug Testing

Advance Notice of Testing				
Number of Tests per Year				
Banned Substances Determination				
Non-random Drug Plan				
Non-positive Drug Violations				

Meeting 6: Final Results

Goal: To finalize decisions for the Collective Bargaining Agreement

Instructions: *(1-1.5 hours)* All members of the UFLPA Union and the Owners Group should be present at this meeting. However, the UFLPA Union Representative and the Owner Representative should serve as the spokesperson for their respective team. This meeting should be conducted much like meeting 4, with the exception of possible strategy alterations from decisions made in meeting 5. The two representatives and the commissioner must sign off on the final contractual agreement points.

Issue	Final Outcome

Salary Cap

Salary Cap DGR Percentage	
Minimum Team Salary	

Benefits

Matching Contribution	
Eligibility For Annuity	
Drug Copay	
Eligibility For Severance Pay	

Conduct

Weight Limit	
Reporting of Injuries	
Late Reporting	
Unexcused Absence	
Loss of Playbook	
Ejection	
Maximum Fine Per Pay Period	

Likeness & Public Appearance

Definition of "Unreasonably"	
Definition of "Representing Clubs"	
Player's Appearance	
Product Endorsements	
Attire	
Criticism / Penalties	

Drug Testing

Advance Notice of Testing	
Number of Tests Per Year	
Banned Substances Determination	
Non-Random Drug Plan	
Non-Positive Drug Violations	

UFLPA Union Representative: _____ Date: _____
UFL Owner Representative: _____ Date: _____
Commissioner: _____ Date: _____

COLLECTIVE BARGAINING AGREEMENT

BETWEEN THE UFL MANAGEMENT COUNCIL AND THE UFL PLAYERS ASSOCIATION

** NOTE: This Collective Bargaining Agreement is an abridged version of the full Agreement found at the NFLPA website. Many sections have been left out or shortened to allow students to focus only on the major issues found in this negotiation. In certain cases, information has been added to this Agreement to aid in simplifying some of the issues and serve as a starting point for negotiations. Each added section is preceded by "**". These added sections are completely the creation of the negotiation designers and should not be taken to be representative of real agreements between the NFL owners and NFLPA.

Introduction

On January 8, 2002, the United Football League Management Council ("Management Council" or "UFLMC") and the United Football League Players Association ("UFLPA") agreed to extend, with certain modifications, the 1993 UFL Collective Bargaining Agreement ("CBA"), which was previously amended June 6, 1996, February 25, 1998, and December 4, 2000. This booklet incorporates the 1998, 2000, and 2002 amendment agreements into the text of the CBA and omits provisions relating exclusively to past seasons (although any such omitted terms, if subsequently determined to be applicable, have the same force and effect as the terms set forth herein. Any persons with questions about provisions concerning seasons before 2002 should refer to prior printed versions of the CBA). The 2000 and 2002 amendment language is set forth in italic copy with applicable notations to the extension agreements. In addition, side letter agreements between the UFLMC and the UFLPA setting forth the parties' interpretation of various provisions of the CBA are reprinted and indented within the appropriate articles. Relevant side letters that were agreed to after the 1998 extension are added to this booklet and are set forth in italics. For easy reference, the article names can be found at the top of each two-page set of this booklet.

Preamble

This Agreement, which is the product of bona fide, arm's length collective bargaining, is made and entered into on the 6th day of May, 1993, in accordance with the provisions of the National Labor Relations Act, as amended, by and between the United Football League Management Council ("Management Council" or "UFLMC"), which is recognized as the sole and exclusive bargaining representative of present and future employer member Clubs of the United Football League ("UFL" or "League"), and the United Football League Players Association ("UFLPA"), which is recognized as the sole and exclusive bargaining representative of present and future employee players in the UFL in a bargaining unit described as follows:

1. All professional football players employed by a member club of the United Football League;

2. All professional football players who have been previously employed by a member club of the United Football League who are seeking employment with an UFL Club;

3. All rookie players once they are selected in the current year's UFL College Draft; and

4. All undrafted rookie players once they commence negotiation with an UFL Club concerning employment as a player.

ARTICLE I: DEFINITIONS

As used in this Agreement, the following terms shall have the following meanings:

Section 1. General Definitions

(a) "Agreement" means this Collective Bargaining Agreement, dated May 6, 1993.

(b) "Class Counsel" means the law firm of Weil, Gotshal & Manges, 767 Fifth Avenue, New York, New York 10153, and the law firm of Lindquist & Vennum, 4200 IDS Center, Minneapolis, Minnesota 55402.

(c) "Club" or "Team" or "Member," used interchangeably herein, means any entity that is a member of the UFL or operates a franchise in the UFL at any time during the term of this Agreement.

(d) "Club Affiliate" or "Team Affiliate" means any entity or person owned by (wholly or partly), controlled by, affiliated with, or related to a Club or any owner of a Club.

(e)   "Commissioner" means the Commissioner of the UFL.

(f)   "Impartial Arbitrator" means the person authorized by this Agreement and the Settlement Agreement to hear and resolve specified disputes as provided in this Agreement and the Settlement Agreement.

(g)   "League Year" means the period from February 20 of one year through and including February 19 of the following year, or such other one year period to which the UFL and the UFLPA may agree.

(h)   "UFL Player Contract" means the form of Player Contract utilized in the UFL.

(i)   "UFL Rules" means the Constitution and By-Laws, rules, and regulations of the UFL and/or the Management Council.

(j)   "Player Affiliate" means any entity or person owned by (wholly or partly), controlled by, affiliated with, or related to a player.

(k)   "Salary" means any compensation of money, property, investments, loans, or anything else of value that a Club pays to, or is obligated to pay to, a player or Player Affiliate, or is paid to a third party at the request of and for the benefit of a player or Player Affiliate, during a League Year, as calculated in accordance with the rules set forth in Article XXIV (Guaranteed League-wide Salary, Salary Cap & Minimum Team Salary).

(l)   "Settlement Agreement" means the Stipulation and Settlement Agreement, dated February 26, 1993.

(m)   "Special Master" means the special master appointed and authorized by this Agreement and the Settlement Agreement to hear and resolve specified disputes as provided in this Agreement and the Settlement Agreement.

Section 2. Free Agency Definitions:

(n)   "Accrued Season" means any playing season for which a player received credit with respect to his qualifications for Unrestricted Free Agency or Restricted Free Agency, as described in Article XIX (Veteran Free Agency).

(o)   "Compensatory Draft Selection" means an additional Draft choice awarded to a Club as described in Article XIX (Veteran Free Agency) and Article XX (Franchise and Transition Players).

(p)   "Draft" or "College Draft" means the UFL's annual draft of Rookie football players as described in Article XVI (College Draft).

(q)   "Draft Choice Compensation" means the right of any Club, as described in Article XIX (Veteran Free Agency) and Article XX (Franchise and Transition Players), to receive draft pick(s) from any other Club.

(r)   "Drafted Rookie" means a person who is selected in the current League Year's Draft or whose Draft rights are held, or continue to be held, consistent with this Agreement, by an UFL Club that selected the Rookie in a prior Draft.

(s)   "Final Eight Plan" means the rules whereby signings of Unrestricted Free Agents are limited in Uncapped Years for the final eight playoff Clubs, under the limited circumstances described in Article XXI (Final Eight Plan).

(t)   "Free Agent" means a player who is not under contract and is free to negotiate and sign a Player Contract with any UFL Club, without Draft Choice Compensation or any Right of First Refusal.

(u)   "Minimum Salary" means the minimum annual Paragraph 5 Salary which shall be paid to an UFL player not on any Active list, and not on the Inactive list, pursuant to this Agreement.

(v)   "Minimum Active/Inactive List Salary" means the minimum annual Paragraph 5 Salary which shall be paid to an UFL player on any Active list, or on the Inactive list, pursuant to this Agreement.

(w) "Negotiate" means, with respect to a player or his representatives on the one hand, and an UFL Club or its representatives on the other hand, to engage in any written or oral communication relating to efforts to reach agreement on employment and/or terms of employment between such player and such Club.

(x) "New Club" means any Club except the Prior Club (as defined below).

(y) "Player Contract" means a written agreement or series of such agreements executed at or about the same time between a person and an UFL Club pursuant to which such person is employed by such Club as a professional football player.

(z) "Prior Club" means the Club that contracted with or otherwise held the UFL playing rights for the player for the previous UFL League Year.

(aa) "Prior Year Salary" means the total of the Paragraph 5 Salary, roster and reporting bonuses, pro-rata portion of signing bonus, and other payments to a player in compensation for the playing of professional football for the last League Year of the player's most recently negotiated Player Contract, except for performance bonuses other than roster and reporting bonuses. Prior Year Salary shall also include any unrepaid loans made, guaranteed or collateralized by a Team or its Team Affiliate to a player or Player Affiliate during or after the 1993 League Year.

(ab) "Renegotiate" means any change in Salary or the terms under which such Salary is earned or paid, or any change regarding the Club's right to trade the player, during the term of a Player Contract.

(ac) "Required Tender" means a Player Contract tender that a Club is required to make to a player pursuant to this Agreement, either as a matter of right with respect to the player, or to receive Rights of First Refusal, Draft Choice Compensation and/or other rights with respect to the player, as specified in this Agreement.

(ad) "Restricted Free Agent" means a Veteran who has three or more Accrued Seasons and who completes performance of his Player Contract, but who is still subject to a Right of First Refusal and/or Draft Choice Compensation in favor of his Prior Club.

(ae) "Right of First Refusal" means the right of an UFL Club, as described in Article XIX (Veteran Free Agency) and Article XX (Franchise and Transition Players) to retain the services of certain Veteran players by matching offers made to those players.

(af) "Rookie" means a person who has never signed a Player Contract with an UFL Club.

(ag) "Undrafted Rookie" means a Rookie who was eligible for but not selected in a College Draft.

(ah) "Unrestricted Free Agent" means a Veteran who completes performance of his Player Contract, and who is no longer subject to any exclusive negotiating rights, Right of First Refusal, or Draft Choice Compensation in favor of his Prior Club.

(ai) "Veteran" means a player who has signed at least one Player Contract with an UFL Club.

Section 3. Salary Cap Definitions:

(aj) "Benefits" or "Player Benefit Costs" means the specific benefits paid to players set forth in Article XXIV (Guaranteed League-wide Salary, Salary Cap & Minimum Team Salary).

(ak) "Capped Year" means any League Year for which a Salary Cap is in effect.

(al) "Defined Gross Revenues" or "DGR" means all of the League and Team revenues that are included within the definition of Defined Gross Revenues, as set forth in Article XXIV (Guaranteed League-wide Salary, Salary Cap & Minimum Team Salary).

(am) "Guaranteed League-wide Salary" means the minimum amount that the Teams in the UFL must pay in Player Costs during a League Year, if applicable, as set forth in Article XXIV (Guaranteed League-wide Salary, Salary Cap & Minimum Team Salary).

(an) "Minimum Team Salary" means the minimum amount that each Team must pay in Salaries during a League Year, if applicable, as set forth in Article XXIV (Guaranteed League-wide Salary, Salary Cap & Minimum Team Salary), Section 5.

(ao) "Paragraph 5 Salary" means the compensation set forth in paragraph 5 of the UFL Player Contract, or in any amendments thereto.

(ap) "Player Costs" means the total Salaries and Benefits attributable to a League Year for all UFL Teams under all of the rules set forth in Article XXIV (Guaranteed League-wide Salary, Salary Cap & Minimum Team Salary), but not including loans, loan guarantees, unpaid grievances attributions, and unearned incentives.

(aq) "Projected Benefits" means the amount of Benefits projected in accordance with the rules set forth in Article XXIV (Guaranteed League-wide Salary, Salary Cap & Minimum Team Salary).

(ar) "Projected Defined Gross Revenues" means the amount of Defined Gross Revenues projected in accordance with the rules set forth in Article XXIV (Guaranteed League-wide Salary, Salary Cap & Minimum Team Salary).

(as) "Room" means the extent to which a Team's then-current Team Salary is less than either the Salary Cap or Entering Player Pool, as applicable.

(at) "Salary Cap" means the absolute maximum amount of Salary that each Club may pay or be obligated to pay or provide to players or Player Affiliates, or may pay or be obligated to pay to third parties at the request of and for the benefit of Players or Player Affiliates, at any time during a particular League Year, in accordance with the rules set forth in Article XXIV (Guaranteed League-wide Salary, Salary Cap & Minimum Team Salary), if applicable.

(au) "Team Salary" means the Team's aggregate Salary for Salary Cap purposes, as calculated in accordance with the rules set forth in Article XXIV (Guaranteed League-wide Salary, Salary Cap & Minimum Team Salary).

(av) "Uncapped Year" means any League Year for which a Salary Cap is not in effect.

Section 4. Further Definitions

(aw) "Final League Year" means the League Year which is scheduled prior to its commencement to be the final League Year of this Agreement. As of the date hereof, the Final League Year is the 2007 League Year. The Final League Year shall always be an Uncapped Year.
*Extension Agreement 1/8/2002

(ax) "Final Capped Year" means the League Year immediately prior to the Final League Year. The Final Capped Year shall be Capped unless the Salary Cap is removed pursuant to Article XXIV (Guaranteed League-wide Salary, Salary Cap & Minimum Team Salary), Section 4(b)(ii)(4).

ARTICLE II: GOVERNING AGREEMENT

Section 1. Conflicts:

The provisions of this Agreement supersede any conflicting provisions in the UFL Player Contract, the UFL Constitution and Bylaws, or any other document affecting terms and conditions of employment of UFL players, and all players, Clubs, the UFLPA, the UFL, and the Management Council will be bound hereby. The provisions of the Stipulation and Settlement Agreement, as amended, in <u>White v. UFL</u>, No. 4-92-906 (D. Minn.) ("Settlement Agreement"), shall supersede any conflicting provisions of this Agreement.

Section 2. Implementation:

The UFLPA and the Management Council will use their best efforts to faithfully carry out the terms and conditions of this Agreement and to see that the terms and conditions of this Agreement are carried out in full by players and Clubs. The UFLPA will use its best efforts to see that the terms and conditions of all UFL Player Contracts are carried out in full by players.

Section 3. Management Rights:

The UFL Clubs maintain and reserve the right to manage and direct their operations in any manner whatsoever, except as specifically limited by the provisions of this Agreement and the Settlement Agreement.

Section 4. Rounding:

For the purposes of any amounts to be calculated or used pursuant to this Agreement with respect to Required Tenders, Qualifying Offers, Minimum Salaries, Minimum Active/Inactive List Salaries, Team Salary, DGR, Excluded DGR, Benefits, Player Costs, Projected DGR, Projected Benefits, or Salary, such amounts shall be rounded to the nearest $1,000.

ARTICLE III: SCOPE OF AGREEMENT

Section 1. Scope:

This Agreement represents the complete understanding of the parties on all subjects covered herein, and there will be no change in the terms and conditions of this Agreement without mutual consent. Except as otherwise provided in Article V (Union Security), Section 6, on Union Security, and on Article LIV (Workers' Compensation), Section 7, on Workers' Compensation, the UFLPA and the Management Council waive all rights to bargain with one another concerning any subject covered or not covered in this Agreement for the duration of this Agreement, including the provisions of the UFL Constitution and Bylaws; provided, however, that if any proposed change in the UFL Constitution and Bylaws during the term of this Agreement could significantly affect the terms and conditions of employment of UFL players, then the Management Council will give the UFLPA notice of and negotiate the proposed change in good faith.

Section 2. Arbitration:

The question of whether the parties engaged in good faith negotiations, or whether any proposed change in the UFL Constitution and Bylaws would violate or render meaningless any provision of this Agreement, may be the subject of a non-injury grievance under Article IX (Non-Injury Grievance), which shall be the exclusive method for resolving disputes arising out of this Section 2. If the arbitrator finds that either party did not engage in good faith negotiations, or that the proposed change would violate or render meaningless any provision of this Agreement, he may enter an appropriate order, including to cease and desist from implementing or continuing the practice or proposal in question;

provided, however, that the arbitrator may not compel either party to this Agreement to agree to anything or require the making of a concession by either party in negotiations.

ARTICLE XXIV: GUARANTEED LEAGUE-WIDE SALARY, SALARY CAP, & MINIMUM TEAM SALARY

Section 1. Definitions:

For purposes of this Article, and anywhere else specifically stated in this Agreement, the following terms shall have the meanings set forth below:

(a)   *Defined Gross Revenues.*

   (i)   "Defined Gross Revenues" (also referred to as "DGR") means the aggregate revenues received or to be received on an accrual basis, for or with respect to a League Year during the term of this Agreement, by the UFL and all UFL Teams (and their designees), from all sources, whether known or unknown, derived from, relating to or arising out of the performance of players in UFL football games, with only the specific exceptions set forth below. The UFL and each UFL Team shall in good faith act and use their best efforts, consistent with sound business judgment, so as to maximize Defined Gross Revenues for each playing season during the term of this Agreement. Defined Gross Revenues shall include, without limitation:

      (1)   Regular season, pre-season, and post-season gate receipts (net of admission taxes, and surcharges paid to stadium or municipal authorities which are deducted for purposes of calculating gate receipts subject to revenue sharing), including ticket revenue from "luxury boxes," suites and premium seating subject to gate receipt sharing among UFL Teams; and

      (2)   Proceeds including Copyright Royalty Tribunal and extended market payments from the sale, license or other conveyance of the right to broadcast or exhibit UFL pre-season, regular season and play-off games on radio and television including, without limitation, network, local, cable, pay television, satellite encryption, international broadcasts, delayed broadcasts (which shall not include any broadcast of an UFL pre-season, regular season or play-off game occurring more than 72 hours after the live exhibition of the game, unless the broadcast is the first broadcast in the market), and all other means of distribution, net of any reasonable and customary UFL expenses related to the project.

      Notwithstanding any other provision of this Agreement, the UFLPA and Class Counsel may agree, on a case-by-case basis, with no limitation on their exercise of discretion, not to include in DGR network television revenue to the extent that such revenue is used to fund the construction or renovation of a stadium that results in an increase of DGR and/or Excluded DGR.
      *Extension Agreement 2/25/98

      (iii)   Notwithstanding subsection 1(a)(i) above, the following shall be considered "Excluded DGR" and not included in Defined Gross Revenues: revenues derived from concessions, parking, local advertising and promotion, signage, magazine advertising, local sponsorship agreements, stadium clubs, luxury box income other than that included in subsection 1(a)(i)(1) above, sales of programs and novelties, and any categories of revenue (other than those listed in subsections 1(a)(i)(l)-(3) above) currently included under UFL Films and UFL Properties, Inc. and its subsidiaries.

(iv)   In calculating Defined Gross Revenues, the amount of Excluded DGR divided by the sum of Excluded DGR plus DGR from all sources except network television revenues shall not exceed the percentage resulting from dividing 1992 Excluded DGR by the sum of 1992 Excluded DGR plus 1992 DGR from all sources except network television revenues. In the event Excluded DGR for any season exceeds the percentage resulting from the above calculation, any excess Excluded DGR shall be included in DGR. For purposes of the calculations described in this subsection (iv), Excluded DGR shall not include any revenues referred to in subsection l(a)(ii).

(v)   Notwithstanding the provisions of subsection 1(a)(i)(2) above, for the purposes of calculating Defined Gross Revenues for the 1993 League Year only, revenues derived from national network television shall be deemed to be $35 million per UFL Team. Any actual amounts received in excess of that amount shall be included pro rata in DGR for the 1994 and 1995 seasons.

(vi)   It is acknowledged by the parties hereto that for purposes of determining Defined Gross Revenues:

    (1)   UFL Teams may, during the term of this Agreement, be owned and controlled by persons or entities that will receive revenues for a grant of rights encompassing both (a) rights from the UFL Team so owned or controlled (the revenue from which is includable in Defined Gross Revenues) and (b) other rights owned or controlled by such persons or entities (the revenue from such other rights not being includable in Defined Gross Revenues), and that, in such circumstances, allocations would therefore have to be made among the rights and revenues described in this Section 1(a); and

    (2)   UFL Teams may, during the term of this Agreement, receive revenue for the grant of rights to third parties which are owned or controlled by the persons or entities owning or controlling such UFL Teams (hereinafter "Related Entities").

(vii)   The reasonableness and includability in DGR of such allocations and transactions between Related Entities shall be determined by the nationally recognized accounting firm jointly retained by the parties, in accordance with the procedures described in Section 10 below.

(viii)   For the purposes of any amounts to be calculated or used pursuant to this Agreement with respect to DGR, Excluded DGR, Benefits, Player Costs, Projected DGR, Projected Benefits, Required Tenders, Qualifying Offers, Minimum Salaries, Minimum Active/Inactive List Salaries, Team Salary, or Salary, such amounts shall be rounded to the nearest $1,000.

(ix)(1) In calculating Defined Gross Revenues, each League Year up to $5 million per year shall be deducted from DGR to the extent that such sums are received that League Year by the UFLPA pursuant to Paragraphs 5, 12, 29 and 30 of the Stipulation and Settlement Agreement in UFLPA v. UFL Properties, Inc., No. 90-CV-4244 (MJL) (S.D.N.Y.).

(ix)(2) In calculating Excluded DGR each League Year, amounts shall be deducted from Excluded DGR to the extent that such sums are received that League Year by any affiliate of the UFLPA, as provided in Paragraph 11 of the Sponsorship Agreement dated January 24, 2001.
    * Extension Agreement 1/8/02

(x)(1)   Without limiting the foregoing, except as specified in subsections (x)(2) through (x)(7) below, DGR shall include all revenues from Personal Seat Licenses ("PSLs") received by, or received by a third party and used, directly or indirectly, for the benefit of, the UFL or any Team or Team Affiliate, without any deduction for taxes or other expenses.

(x)(7)   For purposes of this paragraph, the term "PSL" shall include any and all instruments of any nature, whether of temporary or permanent duration, that give the purchaser the right to acquire or retain tickets to UFL games and shall include, without limitation, seat options and bonds giving purchasers the right to acquire UFL tickets. PSL revenues shall also include revenues from any other device (e.g., periodic payments such as surcharges, loge maintenance fees, etc.) that the UFL and the UFLPA agree constitutes a PSL.

(xi)(6)   For purposes of this paragraph, the term "Premium Seat Revenue" shall include revenue from any periodic charge in excess of the ticket price that is required to be paid to acquire or retain any ticket to UFL games (other than PSL revenues and charges for purchase or rental of luxury suites), including charges in respect of any amenities required to be purchased in connection with any ticket.

(xii)   An amount equal to the lesser of (a) $8 million for each League Year or (b) the amount contributed to or deposited with UFL Charities that League Year by or on behalf of UFL Properties or UFL Films, or any of their subsidiaries, shall be deducted from the calculation of Excluded DGR each such League Year.
* Extension Agreement 1/8/02

(xiii)   Up to the following additional amounts, if committed to youth football programs and contributed by the UFL, its Teams, or their affiliates, in a qualified not-for-profit fund administered by a board jointly appointed by the UFL and the UFLPA, shall also be deducted from the calculation of DGR:

2002 League Year: $20.0 million
2003 League Year: $22.5 million
2004 League Year: $25.0 million
2005 League Year: $25.0 million
2006 League Year: $25.0 million
* Extension Agreement 1/8/02

(xiv)   The parties may agree to allocate DGR received or to be received on an accrual basis in a particular League Year over one or more other League Years.
(xv) If a terrorist or military action occurs after January 8, 2002, with the result that one or more weeks of any UFL season are cancelled or that DGR for any League Year decreases to a catastrophic extent, the parties shall engage in good faith negotiations to adjust the provisions of this Agreement with respect to the projection of DGR and the Salary Cap for the following League Year, so that DGR for the following League Year is projected in a fair manner consistent with the changed revenue projection caused by such action.
* Extension Agreement 1/8/02

(b)   *Benefits.*

"Benefits" and "Player Benefit Costs" mean the aggregate for a League Year of all sums paid (or to be paid on a proper accrual basis for a League Year) by the UFL and all UFL Teams for, to, or on behalf of present or former UFL players, but only for:

(i)   Pension funding, including the Bert Bell/Pete Rozelle UFL Player Retirement Plan (as described in

Article XLVII) and the Second Career Savings Plan (as described in Article XLVIII); provided that all costs associated with the benefit increase, to which the parties agreed in 2002, under Article XLVII, Section 8, shall be allocated for Player Benefit Costs purposes in equal amounts to the 2002-2006 League Years;

(ii)   Group insurance programs, including, life, medical, and dental coverage (as described in Article XLIX or as required by law), and the Supplemental Disability Plan (as described in Article LI);

(iii)   Injury protection (as described in Article XII);

(iv)   Workers' compensation, payroll, unemployment compensation, and social security taxes;

(iv)   Preseason per diem amounts (as described in Sections 3 and 4 of Article XXXVII) and regular season meal allowances (as described in Article XXXIX);

(v)   Moving and travel expenses (as described in Sections 2, 3, and 4 of Article XLI, and Section 8 of Article XXXVII);

(vii)   Postseason pay (as described in Article XLII and Article XLIII); and salary paid to practice squad players pursuant to a practice squad contract during the postseason, unless the practice squad player contract is executed or renegotiated after December 1 for more than the minimum practice squad salary, in which case all salary paid to such a practice squad player during the postseason will be counted as Salary.

(viii)   Player medical costs (i.e., fees to doctors, hospitals, and other health care providers, and the drugs and other medical cost of supplies, for the treatment of player injuries), but not including salaries of trainers or other Team personnel, or the cost of Team medical or training equipment (in addition, the amount of player medical costs included in Benefits may not increase by more than ten percent (10%) each League Year);

(ix)   Severance pay (as described in Article L);

(x)   The Player Annuity Program (as described in Article XLVIII-A);

(xi)   The (as described in Article XXXVIII-A);

(xii)   The Performance Based Pool (as described in Article XXXVIII-B); and

(xiii)   The Tuition Assistance Plan (as described in Article XLVIII-B).
    * Extension Agreement 1/8/02

Benefits will not include salary reduction contributions elected by a player to the Second Career Savings Plan described in Article XLVIII. Benefits also will not include any tax imposed on the UFL or UFL Clubs pursuant to section 4972 of the Internal Revenue Code for the Bert Bell/Pete Rozelle UFL Player Retirement Plan. Benefits for a League Year will be determined by adding together all payments made and amounts properly accrued by or on behalf of the UFL and all UFL Clubs for the above purposes during that League Year, except that Benefits for pension funding and the Second Career Savings Plan will be deemed to be made in a League Year for purposes of this Article if made in the Plan Year beginning in the same calendar year as the beginning of such League Year.

(c)   *Salary.*

(i)   "Salary" means the compensation in money, property, investments, loans or anything else of value to which an UFL player (including Rookie and Veteran players and players whose contracts have been terminated) or his Player Affiliate is entitled in accordance with a Player Contract, but not including Benefits. Salary with respect to any period shall include all Salary actually payable with respect to such period under the terms of a Player Contract and all Salary attributable to such period under the terms of this Agreement.

(ii)   A player's Salary shall also include any and all consideration received by the player or his Player Affiliate, even if such consideration is ostensibly paid to the player for services other than football playing services, if the UFL can demonstrate before the Impartial Arbitrator that the consideration paid to the player or Player Affiliate for such non-football services does not represent a reasonable approximation of the fair market value of such services as performed by such player. The Impartial Arbitrator's determination may take into account, among other things: (1) any actual dollar amounts the player or Player Affiliate received for similar non-football playing services from an independent third party; and (2) the percentage of total compensation for non-football services received from third parties versus the Team or Team Affiliate.

(iii)   For purposes of this Article, Salary shall be computed pursuant to the additional rules below.

Section 2. Trigger for Guaranteed League-wide Salary, Salary Cap, and Minimum Team Salary:

There shall be no Guaranteed League-wide Salary, Salary Cap, or Minimum Team Salary for UFL Teams during the 1993 League Year. If in the 1993 League Year or any subsequent League Year the total Player Costs for all UFL Teams equals or exceeds 67% of actual Defined Gross Revenues, there shall be a Guaranteed League-wide Salary, Salary Cap, and Minimum Team Salary in the amounts set forth below for the next League Year and all subsequent League Years, unless the Salary Cap is removed pursuant to Section 4(b)(ii)(4) below. Notwithstanding the immediately preceding sentence, there will be no Guaranteed League-wide Salary, Salary Cap or Minimum Team Salary in the Final League Year.

Section 3. Guaranteed League-wide Salary:

In any League Year in which a Salary Cap is in effect there shall be a Guaranteed League-wide Salary of 58% of actual Defined Gross Revenues. In the event that the Player Costs for all UFL Teams during any League Year in which a Salary Cap is in effect are less than 58% of actual Defined Gross Revenues for such season, then, on or before April 15 of the next League Year, the UFL shall pay an amount equal to such deficiency directly to players who played on UFL Teams during such season pursuant to the reasonable allocation instructions of the UFLPA.

Section 4. Salary Cap Amounts:

(a)   Subject to the adjustments set forth below, the amount of the Salary Cap for each UFL Team in years that it is in effect shall be (1) in the 2002 League Year, 64% of the Projected Defined Gross Revenues, less League-wide Projected Benefits, divided by the number of Teams playing in the UFL during such year; (2) in the 2003 League Year, 64.25% of the Projected Defined Gross Revenues, less League-wide Projected Benefits, divided by the number of Teams playing in the UFL during such year; (3) in the 2004 League Year, 64.75% of the Projected Defined Gross Revenues, less League-wide Projected Benefits, divided by the number of Teams playing in the UFL during such year; (4) in the 2005 League Year, 65.5% of the Projected Defined Gross Revenues, less League-wide Projected Benefits, divided by the number of Teams playing in the UFL during such year; and (5) in the 2006 League Year, 64.5% of the Projected Defined Gross Revenues, less League-wide Projected Benefits, divided by the number of Teams playing in the UFL during such year. Notwithstanding the foregoing, the UFLPA or the UFL may, by providing written notice on or before December 1, 2004, move one half of a percentage point from the 2005 League Year to the 2006 League Year so that the Salary Cap in each of the 2005 and 2006 League Years shall be 65% of the Projected Defined Gross Revenues, less League-wide Projected Benefits, divided by the number of Teams playing in the UFL during that year.
* Extension Agreement 1/8/02
* Wherever the parties have agreed that a difference in the Salary Cap is to be carried over into a future League Year (e.g., Article XXIV, Section 10(a)(ii)), if the number of Clubs in the UFL changes from the League Year

in which the Salary Cap difference originated to the League Year in which it will be applied, the amount of the difference will be adjusted to reflect the different number of Clubs in the UFL.
* Side Letter 10/20/98

(b)   The foregoing Salary Cap amounts shall be adjusted as follows:

    (i)   The actual dollar amount of the Salary Cap shall not be less than the actual dollar amount of any Salary Cap in effect during the preceding League Year; provided, however, that at no time shall the Projected Benefits, plus the amount of the Salary Cap multiplied by the number of Teams in the UFL, exceed 70% of the Projected Defined Gross Revenues.

    (ii)   If the total Player Costs of the UFL Teams during any League Year in which the Salary Cap is in effect falls below:

        (1)   59% of actual Defined Gross Revenues, then the Salary Cap percentage for the next League Year shall be increased by 1% of Projected Defined Gross Revenues;

        (2)   58% of actual Defined Gross Revenues, then the Salary Cap percentage for the next League Year shall be increased by 2% of Projected Defined Gross Revenues;

        (3)   57% of actual Defined Gross Revenues, then the Salary Cap percentage for the next League Year shall be increased by 3% of Projected Defined Gross Revenues;

        (4)   56% of actual Defined Gross Revenues, then there shall be no Salary Cap for the next League Year or any succeeding League Year unless and until the Salary Cap again becomes effective in accordance with Section 2 of this Article.

(c)   If, by January 15, 2005, no extension of the term of this Agreement has been agreed to by the parties and the 2006 League Year is then scheduled to be the Final Capped Year, Article XXIV, Section 4(b)(i) shall not apply to the 2006 League Year. If, by January 15, 2005, the parties have agreed to extend the term of this Agreement, so that the 2006 League Year will not be the Final Capped Year, Article XXIV, Section 4(b)(i) shall continue to apply to the 2006 League Year and all Capped Years of any extended term. An example reflecting application of Article XXIV, Section 4(b)(i), if such provision were to apply in the 2006 League Year, is annexed hereto as Exhibit O.

(d)   Reasonable security expenses incurred at both the Club and League level the prior League Year, to the extent that they exceed such expenses for the 2000 League Year (plus 5% each year for inflation for such expenses), shall be multiplied by the Salary Cap percentage for the applicable League Year, and the resulting amount shall be deducted from the calculation of the Salary Cap, up to a maximum of $250,000 per Club in any League Year, with no carryover into future League Years. For each such League Year, the Management Council shall present to the UFLPA a reasonable estimate of such incremental expenses, and the parties shall negotiate in good faith to determine the appropriate deduction.

(e)

    (i)   For each Capped Year, if the percentage resulting from the "Cash Salary" paid to players (as defined below) that League Year, divided by DGR for that League Year, averaged for that League Year and the prior two League Years (i.e., three-year rolling average), exceeds 71.5%, the UFL will receive a Salary Cap Credit equal to the difference in these percentages multiplied by the amount of DGR for that League Year. The credit shall be used in the Capped Year immediately following the League Year in which the credit arose (subject to any application of Article XXIV, Section 4(b)(i)), but any unused credit can be carried over to future Capped Years (subject to any application of Article XXIV, Section 4(b)(i)). For example, if the rolling average calculated in a given League Year is 72.5% and DGR for that League Year is $3.2 billion, the amount of the Salary Cap Credit arising from that League Year would be equal to a total of $32 million (i.e., $1 million per team if there are 32 teams in the UFL).

    (ii)   "Cash Salary" for purposes of this subparagraph is the sum of total Paragraph 5 amounts earned by players (applying the valuation rules which apply to deferred salary specified in Article XXIV, Section 7(a)(ii)), signing bonus amounts paid or committed (including amounts treated as signing bonus pursuant to this Agreement), incentives that have been earned and paid, or earned and committed to be paid to players (applying the valuation rules which apply to deferred salary specified in Article XXIV, Section 7(a)(ii)), grievances settled, termination pay, injury settlements, Salary advances that were not included in Paragraph 5, and anything else paid or provided to players during that League Year that would be valued under the Salary Cap (e.g., the fair market value of automobiles gifted to players).

(iii)   The Cash Salary percentages shall be deemed to be 71.6% for the 1999 League Year and 68.3% for the 2000 League Year.
          * Extension Agreement 1/8/02

Section 5. Minimum Team Salary:

With respect to each League Year for which a Salary Cap is in effect, there shall be a guaranteed Minimum Team Salary of 56% of Projected Defined Gross Revenues, less League-wide Projected Benefits, divided by the then current number of Teams in the UFL. Each Team shall be required to have a Team Salary of at least the Minimum Team Salary at the end of each League Year.
* Extension Agreement 1/8/02 [prior League Year percentages omitted]

(b)   Nothing contained herein shall preclude a Team from having a Team Salary in excess of the Minimum Team Salary, provided it does not exceed the Salary Cap.

(c)   Any shortfall in the Minimum Team Salary at the end of a League Year shall be paid, on or before April 15 of the next League Year, by the Teams having such shortfall, directly to the players who were on such Teams' roster at any time during the season, pursuant to reasonable allocation instructions of the UFLPA.

(d)   If the UFL agrees, or a judgment or award is entered by the Special Master, that a Team has failed by the end of the then current League Year to make the payments required to satisfy a Team's obligations to pay the Minimum Team Salary required by this Agreement, then, in the event the Team fails promptly to comply with such agreement, judgment or award, the UFL shall make such payment on behalf of that Team (such funds to be paid as salary directly to the players on such Team at the direction of and pursuant to the reasonable allocation

ARTICLE XLVI: PLAYER BENEFIT COSTS

Section 1:

(b)   **1998 Amendment Benefits:** During each League Year for which a Salary Cap applies, the UFLPA will have the unilateral right to increase, reduce or freeze each separate and individual Player Benefit Cost relating to 1998 Amendment Benefits that are set forth in Sections 5(c), 5(d) and 5(e) of this Article to the extent permitted by law, to ensure that the total cost of the 1998 Amendment Benefits does not exceed and is not less than the amount set forth below for each such League Year. Any increase shall be for one League Year only and shall not create a continuing obligation for the Clubs. The total cost of the 1998 Amendment Benefits for Capped Years in the 2002 League Year and thereafter shall be $100 million, plus an additional amount, if necessary, sufficient to raise the Allocation under the Player Annuity Program to $65,000 for each player eligible for an Allocation, unless the parties agree otherwise.

Section 2. Right of Restoration:

Each separate and individual benefit reduced or frozen pursuant to Section 1 above may be unilaterally restored by the UFLPA in whole or in part for a League Year, if such right is exercised on or before April 15 of such League Year. Each benefit may be restored up to but not in excess of its prescribed level for that League Year in this Agreement.

Section 3. Definition:

For purposes of this Agreement, the term "Player Benefit Costs," as also set forth in Article XXIV (Guaranteed League-wide Salary, Salary Cap & Minimum Team Salary) means the aggregate for a League Year of all sums paid (or to be paid on a proper accrual basis for a League Year) by the UFL and all UFL Clubs for, to or on behalf of present or former UFL players, but only for:

(a) Pension funding, including the Bert Bell/Pete Rozelle UFL Player Retirement Plan (as described in Article XLVII) and the Second Career Savings Plan (as described in Article XLVIII); provided that all costs associated with the benefit increase, to which the parties agreed in 2002, under Article XLVII, Section 8, shall be allocated for Player Benefit Costs purposes in equal amounts to the 2002-2006 League Years;

(b) Group insurance programs, including, life, medical, and dental coverage (as described in Article XLIX or as required by law), and the Supplemental Disability Plan (as described in Article LI);

(c) Injury protection (as described in Article XII);

(d) Workers' compensation, payroll, unemployment compensation, and social security taxes;

(e) Pre-season per diem amounts (as described in Sections 3 and 4 of Article XXXVII) and regular season meal allowances (as described in Article XXXIX);

(f) Moving and travel expenses (as described in Sections 2, 3, and 4 of Article XLI, and Section 8 of Article XXXVII);

(g) Postseason pay (as described in Article XLII and Article XLIII); and salary paid to practice squad players pursuant to a practice squad contract during the postseason, unless the practice squad player contract is executed or renegotiated after December 1 for more than the minimum practice squad salary, in which case all salary paid to such a practice squad player during the postseason will be counted as Salary;

(h) Player medical costs (i.e., fees to doctors, hospitals, and other health care providers, and the drugs and other medical cost of supplies, for the treatment of player injuries), but not including salaries of trainers or other Team personnel, or the cost of Team medical or training equipment (in addition, the amount of player medical costs included in Player Benefit Costs may not increase more than ten percent (10%) each League Year, beginning with the 1993 League Year);

(i) Severance pay (as described in Article L);

(j) The Player Annuity Program (as described in Article XLVIII-A);

(k) The Minimum Salary Benefit (as described in Article XXXVIII-A);

(l) The Performance Based Pool (as described in Article XXXVIII-B); and

(m) The Tuition Assistance Plan (as described in Article XLVIII-B).
Extension Agreement 1/8/02

Player Benefit Costs will not include salary reduction contributions elected by a player to the Second Career Savings Plan described in Article XLVIII, and such salary reduction contributions will not reduce Player Salaries for purposes of Article XXIV.

Section 6. Limitations on Contributions:

Effective March 1, 2002,

(a) No UFL club shall have any obligation, directly or indirectly, to contribute to the Second Career Savings Plan, the Supplemental Disability Plan, the Player Annuity Program, the Severance Pay Plan, or the Tuition

Assistance Plan (individually, a "Player Benefit Plan") with respect to an Uncapped Year except to the extent required by the Internal Revenue Code. Each Player Benefit Plan shall be amended to prevent any employer provided benefit from accruing or being otherwise credited, paid, or earned thereunder with respect to an Uncapped Year, and to provide that no expense incurred in maintaining the Player Benefit Plan in an Uncapped Year shall be paid, directly or indirectly, by an UFL Club. During an Uncapped Year, a payment of benefits under a Player Benefit Plan shall be made only if and to the extent the payment either is funded, or is required by ERISA.

ARTICLE XLVII: RETIREMENT PLAN

Section 1. Maintenance and Definitions:

The Bert Bell/Pete Rozelle UFL Player Retirement Plan (the "Bert Bell/Pete Rozelle Plan" or "Merged Plan") will be continued and maintained in full force and effect during the term of this Agreement.

Section 3. Contributions:

For the 1993 Plan Year and continuing for each Plan Year thereafter that begins prior to the expiration of the Final League Year, a contribution will be made to the Bert Bell Plan, the Pete Rozelle Plan, or the Merged Plan, as appropriate, on behalf of each UFL Club as actuarially determined to be necessary to fund the benefits provided in this Article, based on the actuarial assumptions and methods contained in Appendix J.

Credited Season In Plan Year	Benefit Credit
Before 1982	$200
1982 through 1992	230
1993 and 1994	240
1995 and 1996	285
1997	330
1998 through Plan Year that begins prior to the expiration of final League Year	425

Section 6. Medical Standards for Line-of-Duty Disability Benefits:

The parties agree to amend the Bert Bell/Pete Rozelle Plan to adopt revised medical standards for Line-of-Duty disability benefits based upon the American Medical Association's Guides to the Evaluation of Permanent Impairment (Fourth Edition, Chicago, IL) ("AMA Guides"). Effective for applications received on and after April 1, 2002, the parties will amend Section 6.4 of the Bert Bell/Pete Rozelle Plan to read substantially as follows:
"6.4 Definitions
(a)A "substantial disablement" is a "permanent" disability that
(1)Results in a 50% or greater loss of speech or sight; or
(2) Results in a 55% or greater loss of hearing; or
(3) Is the primary or contributory cause of the surgical removal or major functional impairment of a vital bodily organ or part of the central nervous system; or
(4) For orthopedic impairments, using the Guides to the Evaluation of Permanent Impairment (Fourth Edition, Chicago, IL), is (a) a 55% or greater loss of use of the entire lower extremity; or (b) a 30% or greater loss of use of the

entire upper extremity; or (c) an impairment to the spine that results in a 29% or greater whole body impairment. In each case for orthopedic impairments, a maximum of 10 percentage points will be allowed for symptoms of pain."
*Extension Agreement 1/8/02

ARTICLE XLVIII: SECOND CAREER SAVINGS PLAN

Section 2. Contributions:

(a) **Prior to 2001:** For each of the Plan Years 1993 through 1999, a contribution of $215,000 will be made to the Savings Plan on behalf of each UFL Club. For the 2000 Plan Year, a contribution of $250,000 will be made to the Savings Plan on behalf of each Club. Such contributions will be made in four (4) equal payments, on June 30, September 30, December 31, and March 31 of each such Plan Year.
*Extension Agreement 2/25/98, as amended by Extension Agreement 1/8/02

(b) **2001 and Later Years:** For each of the Plan Years 2001 and thereafter in which the Salary Cap applies, a contribution will be made to the Savings Plan on behalf of each UFL Club as follows:

    (i) **Matching Contributions.** The parties will amend the Savings Plan to require the UFL Clubs in the aggregate to contribute a matching amount for each player who earns a Credited Season during such Plan Year, who would qualify for a Minimum Contribution under (ii) below if Matching Contributions were not made on his behalf, and who makes a salary reduction contribution to the Savings Plan ("Matching Contribution"). The amount of such Matching Contribution shall be two Dollars (up to a maximum of $20,000) for each dollar contributed by the player. Any salary reduction contribution made by a player to the Savings Plan during a calendar year will be eligible to be matched in the Plan Year that begins during such calendar year. The UFL Clubs will be required to contribute the Matching Contribution:

        (a) by December 1 of such Plan Year for those players who (i) earn a Credited Season by and through the sixth week of the regular season and (ii) make a salary reduction contribution of $10,000 or more to the Savings Plan for that calendar year by the end of the first full week in November of such Plan Year; and

        (b) by the last day of such Plan Year (March 31 of the following calendar year) for all other eligible players.

    (ii) **Minimum Contribution.** The UFL Clubs in the aggregate will contribute to the Savings Plan, for each Plan Year in which a Salary Cap applies, a contribution of at least $3,600 for each player who earns a Credited Season during such Plan Year and has three or more Credited Seasons, and $7,200 for each player who earns a Credited Season during such Plan Year and has exactly two Credited Seasons ("Minimum Contribution"). Any Matching Contribution made on behalf of a player will reduce his Minimum Contribution on a dollar-for-dollar basis (but not below zero). Any and all Minimum Contributions that are not Matching Contributions described in Subsection (b)(i) above shall be made by and as of the last day of the Plan Year.

    (iii) Expenses. The UFL Clubs will make contributions to the Savings Plan at least quarterly in an amount sufficient to pay administrative expenses.

Section 3. Expansion of Eligible Employees:

Effective as of April 1, 2002, the parties will amend the Savings Plan so that first year players (not including practice squad players) may participate and contribute to the Savings Plan, but will not receive employer contributions under Sections 3.2, 3.3, 3.4, or 3.6 of the Savings Plan for that Plan Year.
*Extension Agreement 1/8/02

ARTICLE XLVIII – A: PLAYER ANNUITY PROGRAM

Section 2. Contributions:

For each of the Annuity Years 2001 and thereafter in which a Salary Cap applies, a contribution will be made to the Player Annuity Program on behalf of the UFL Clubs unless this figure is changed pursuant to this Agreement, including the rights of the parties under Section 1(b) of Article XLVI of this Agreement, in the amount of $73 million, but not less than an amount sufficient to fund an Allocation of $65,000 to each player eligible for an Allocation, unless the parties agree otherwise.
* Extension Agreement 1/8/02

Contributions to the Player Annuity Program for an Annuity Year will be made as follows:

> 1. Expenses: The UFL Clubs will prepay contributions to the Annuity Program at least quarterly in an amount sufficient to pay administrative expenses. For purposes of this provision the term "administrative expenses" does not include reserve or similar capital requirements.

> 2. Allocations: Allocations for the benefit of individual players will be made on and as of December 31 and March 31 of each Annuity Year, as described in Section 3(c) below.

Section 3. Eligibility and Allocation:

(a) **Points:** For Annuity Year 2001 and each year thereafter for which a Salary Cap applies, players who earn a Credited Season, as that term is defined in the Bert Bell/Pete Rozelle Plan, in an Annuity Year and who have a total of four or more Credited Seasons as of the end of such Annuity Year will receive one point for each such Credited Season.

(b) **Individual Allocations:** The amount allocated to an individual player who receives a point in the 2001 and later Annuity Years will be calculated as follows: In December of each such year a good faith estimate will be made by the Annuity Board of the total contribution expected to be made during such Annuity Year under Section 2 above by all UFL Clubs, minus the estimated administrative expenses for the Annuity Year, and minus any retroactive allocations made to players under rules similar to those in Section 3.4 of the Savings Plan. A good faith estimate will also be made at that time by the Annuity Board of the total points expected to be earned during such Annuity Year by all players. The value of a point will be determined by (1) taking the total estimated available contributions as described above and (2) dividing by the estimate of the total points expected to be earned by all players. The Allocation to each player eligible for an Allocation will, for each of the 2002 through 2006 Annuity Years, not be less than $65,000, unless the parties agree otherwise.
*Extension Agreement 1/8/02

(c) **Timing:** Eligible players who earn a Credited Season by December 1 of an Annuity Year will receive their allocation on December 31 of such Annuity Year. All other players who are entitled to an allocation in an Annuity Year will receive their allocation on March 31 of such Annuity Year.

Section 4. Distributions:

A player may elect to begin receiving distributions under the Player Annuity Program in the form of annuity or installment payments at any time after the later of (a) the player's attainment of age 35, or (b) five years after the end of the Annuity Year containing the player's last Credited Season. Payments must begin no later than age 65. A player who elects to begin receiving annuity or installment payments under the preceding sentences may elect to receive such payments in substantially equal amounts for a period beginning on the date of commencement of such payments and ending upon the player's attainment of age 45, or such later age as he shall specify, or for life. Alternatively, a player may elect to defer his receipt of distributions under the Player Annuity Program. Upon a player's attainment of age 45, such player may elect to receive his benefit under the Player Annuity Program in the form of an annuity or a lump sum payment. If a player dies before making an election to receive benefits, the player's named beneficiary may make an election that otherwise would have been available to the player. A player's rights under the Player Annuity Program may not be transferred, assigned, or alienated.

ARTICLE XLVIII-B: TUITION ASSISTANCE PLAN

Section 1. Establishment:

Effective April 1, 2002, the parties shall establish a new benefit program to be called the UFL Player Tuition Assistance Plan. The Plan will provide up to $15,000 per League year as reimbursement for tuition, fees, and books to any player who earns an average of "C" or better per semester at an eligible educational institution within the meaning of Section 529(e)(5) of the Internal Revenue Code. To be eligible for reimbursement, fees must be associated with the course or courses taken, and no more than $400 in fees will be reimbursed for any semester. The Plan Year for the Tuition Assistance Plan will begin on April 1.

Section 2. Eligibility:

To be eligible for reimbursement in any League Year, the player must have earned at least one Credited Season prior to the beginning of an academic year and (i) be on the Active, Inactive, or Reserve/Injured roster for the first game of the UFL regular season for reimbursement for the Fall semester during that UFL season, or (ii) be on the Active, Inactive, or Reserve/Injured roster for the last game of the UFL regular season for reimbursement for any other semester during that academic year.

Section 3. Reimbursement:

An eligible player will be reimbursed by no more than seventy five (75) days after the player submits a certified transcript from the eligible educational institution for that semester, and receipts demonstrating payment for tuition, fees, or books.

ARTICLE XLIX: GROUP INSURANCE

Section 1. Group Insurance Benefits:

Players will receive group insurance benefits, consisting of life insurance, medical, and dental benefits, as follows:

(a) **Life Insurance:** For the 2002-06 League Years, a rookie player will be entitled to $150,000 in coverage, and a veteran player's coverage will be increased by $30,000 for each Credited Season (as defined by the Bert Bell/Pete Rozelle Plan) up to a maximum of $300,000 in coverage.

(b) **Medical:** Until and including August 31, 2002, each player is required to pay an annual deductible of $200 per individual per plan year and $400 per family per plan year, with a maximum out-of-pocket expense of $800 per plan year (including the deductible) for each covered individual. Effective September 1, 2002, each player is required to pay an annual deductible of $400 per individual per plan year and $800 per family per plan year, with a maximum out-of-pocket expense of $1600 (including the deductible) for each covered individual. Effective March 1, 2002,

1) the co-insurance paid by a covered individual for services rendered by out-of-network providers will change from 20% of covered charges to 30% of covered charges; and

2) the amount paid by a covered individual for non-compliance with pre-certification and emergency admission procedures will be $500 and the reimbursement paid to the covered individual for such services shall be reduced by 50%; and

3) a prescription drug card will be provided to covered individuals requiring a $5 co-pay for generic drugs and a $10 co-pay for brand name drugs if the generic or brand name drugs are obtained from participating pharmacies. The availability of participating pharmacies will not be significantly reduced below the level initially provided by CIGNA.

4) Notwithstanding the effective date stated above, the maximum lifetime benefits paid on behalf of a covered individual will be $2.5 million effective September 9, 2001.

(d) **Insurance Benefits for Vested Players:** Players vested under the Bert Bell/Pete Rozelle Plan who are released or otherwise sever employment on or before May 1 in a calendar year will continue to receive insurance coverage under this Article until the first regular season game of the season that begins later in that calendar year. Players vested under the Bert Bell/Pete Rozelle Plan who are released or otherwise sever employment after May 1 in a calendar year will continue to receive insurance coverage under this Article until the first regular season game of the season that begins in the following calendar year. Group insurance benefits are guaranteed during the term of this Agreement unless reduced by the UFLPA pursuant to Article XLVI (Player Benefit Costs), Section 1, or required to be modified by law.

(e) **Family Medical and Dental Coverage for Deceased Players:** A player's enrolled dependents (including a child born to the player's wife within ten months after the player's death) shall be entitled to continuing family medical and dental insurance coverage effective August 1, 2001, as follows:

1) for the dependents of a player on the Active, Inactive, Reserve/ Injured, Reserve/PUP, or Practice Squad roster at the time of the player's death, coverage will continue for the length of time the player would have been covered had his contract been terminated on the date of his death for any reason other than death;

2) for dependents of a player who was receiving coverage under Section 1(d) , 2(c), or 2(d) of this Article at the time of his death, coverage will continue for the remaining length of time that the player would have been eligible under such Section had his death not occurred.
*Extension Agreement 1/8/02

Section 5. Administration:

The Management Council will assume administrative responsibility for group insurance benefits. The UFLPA will have the right to veto for cause any insurance company or other entity selected by the UFL or the Management Council to provide benefits under this Article. Reasons justifying such a veto for cause include, but are not limited to, excessive cost, poor service, or insufficient financial reserves. The parties agree to review and consider the most cost efficient manner to provide the coverage described in this Article. Upon request by the UFLPA, the Management Council will promptly provide the UFLPA with any document or other information relating to group insurance, including materials relating to experience and costs.

ARTICLE L: SEVERANCE PAY

Section 1. Eligibility:

Only players with two or more Credited Seasons (as that term is defined in the Bert Bell/Pete Rozelle Plan), at least one of which is for a season occurring in 1993 through *2006,* will be eligible for severance pay under this Article. Except as provided in Section 8, this Article will not extinguish or affect any other rights that a player may have to any other severance pay.

Section 2. Amount:

Each eligible player will receive severance pay in the amounts determined as follows: (a) $5,000 per Credited Season for each of the seasons 1989 through 1992; (b) $10,000 per Credited Season for each of the seasons 1993 through 1999; (c) $12,500 per Credited Season for each of the seasons 2000 through 2006.
* Extension Agreement 1/8/02

Section 3. Application:

To apply for severance pay under this Article, a player must submit a request in writing to the UFL Club that he was under contract with when he earned his last Credited Season, with copies to the Executive Director of the UFLPA and the Executive Vice President for Labor Relations of the UFL. His request must indicate his intention to permanently sever employment with all UFL Clubs as an Active Player.

Section 4. Payment:

Severance pay under this Article will be paid in a single lump sum payment by the UFL Club with which the player last earned a Credited Season according to the following schedule:

LAST LEAGUE PLAYING ACTIVITY	IF APPLY NO LATER THAN	PAYMENT DATE
The date of the first regular season game of that player's Club through League Week 8, or earlier	March 1	March 31
League Week 9 through the end of the League Year, or earlier	June 1	June 30
The beginning of the League Year through May 31, or earlier	September 1	September 30
June 1 through the date immediately preceding the date of the first regular season game of that player's Club, or earlier	December 1	December 31

Section 5. Failure to Apply:

A player who has not applied for severance pay under this Article within twenty (20) months of his last participation in UFL football playing activities will be deemed to have applied under this Article as of the expiration date of such twenty (20) month period.

Section 6. Only One Payment:

Any player who returns to UFL football after receiving a severance payment under this Article will not be entitled to any further severance pay.

Section 7. Payable to Survivor:

In the event a player eligible to receive severance pay under this Article dies before receiving such pay, the player's designated beneficiary (or his estate in the absence of a designated beneficiary) will be entitled to receive such pay on the later of (a) the next payment date following the date of the player's death, or (b) thirty (30) days after written notification of the player's death.

Article VIII: CLUB DISCIPLINE

Section 1. Maximum Discipline:

(a)   For the 1993 League Year, the following maximum discipline schedule will be applicable:
Overweight-maximum fine of $50 per lb./per day.

Failure to promptly report injury to Club physician or trainer-maximum fine of $200.

Losing, damaging or altering Club-provided equipment-maximum fine of $200 and replacement cost, if any.

Throwing football into stands-maximum fine of $200.

Unexcused late reporting for or absence from pre-season training camp by a player under contract … pursuant to Article XIX (Veteran Free Agency)-maximum fine of $4,000 per day for the 1993-95 League years, $5,000 per day for the 1996-2004 League Years and $6,000 per day for the 2005-07 League Years, plus one week's regular season salary for each pre-season game missed.

Unexcused missed mandatory off-season training camp, team meeting, practice, curfew, bed check, scheduled appointment with Club physician or trainer, material failure to follow Club rehabilitation directions, or scheduled promotional activity-maximum fine of $1,000.

Material failure to follow rehabilitation program prescribed by Club physician or trainer-maximum fine of $1,000.

Unexcused missed team transportation-maximum fine of $1,000 and transportation expense, if any.

Loss of all or part of playbook, scouting report or game plan-maximum fine of $1,000.

Ejection from game-maximum fine of $2,000.

Conduct detrimental to Club-maximum fine of an amount equal to one week's salary and/or suspension without pay for a period not to exceed four (4) weeks.

The Club will promptly notify the player of any discipline.

Section 2. Published Lists:

All Clubs must publish and make available to all players at the commencement of pre-season training camp a complete list of the discipline which can be imposed for designated offenses within the limits set by the maximum schedule referred to in Section 1 above.

Section 3. Uniformity:

Discipline will be imposed uniformly within a Club on all players for the same offense; however, the Club may specify the events which create an escalation of the discipline, provided the formula for escalation is uniform in its application. Any disciplinary action imposed upon a player by the Commissioner pursuant to Article XI (Commissioner Discipline) will preclude or supersede disciplinary action by the Club for the same act or conduct.

Section 5. Deduction:

Any Club fine will be deducted at the rate of no more than $1,000 from each pay period, if sufficient pay periods remain; or, if less than sufficient pay periods remain, the fine will be deducted in equal installments over the number of remaining pay periods. This will not apply to a suspension.

Article V

Section 4. UFLPA Player Group Licensing Program:

The UFL recognizes that players have authorized the UFLPA to act as their agent in a Group Player Licensing program (defined below) for their benefit. … Any disputes that arise regarding the UFL's conduct in this regard shall be submitted for expedited arbitration pursuant to Article IX (Non-Injury Grievance). For the purposes of this Section 4, Group Player Licensing shall be defined as the use of a total of six or more UFL players' names, signatures facsimiles, voices, pictures, photographs, likenesses and/or biographical information on or in conjunction with products (including, but not limited to, trading cards, clothing, videogames, computer games, collectibles, internet sites, fantasy games, etc.): (a) in any one product category, as defined by industry standards; or (b) in different categories if a total of six or more players are used and (i) the products all use similar or derivative design or artwork or (ii) one such player product is used to promote another player product. For the purposes of this Section 4, Group Player Licensing includes, without limitation, products sold at retail and products that are used as promotional or premium items.
*Extension Agreement 1/8/02

Article VII

Section 2. Personal Appearance:

Clubs may make and enforce reasonable rules governing players' appearance on the field and in public places while representing the Clubs; provided, however, that no player will be disciplined because of hair length or facial hair.

**Representing clubs is taken to mean any team-sponsored activities including, but not limited to: games, promotional appearances, media involvement, and team travel. **

Article LV

Section 1. Endorsements:

No Club may unreasonably refuse to permit a player to endorse a product.

Section 2. On-Field Attire:

Neither the UFL nor any of the Clubs may have any rule prohibiting or limiting the type of footwear or gloves which may be worn by players on the field, except to the extent such rules or limitations are agreed to by the UFLPA.

Section 3. Appearances:

No Club may unreasonably require a player to appear on radio or television.

**Reasonable requirements are defined as follows: two hours before and after a game on game days, all other days of the week excluding holidays not listed in this section, Christmas, and Thanksgiving. These requirements apply year round (i.e. in-season and out-of-season). **

Section 4. Promotion:

The UFLPA will use its best efforts to ensure that the players cooperate with the Clubs and the news media in reasonable promotional activities on behalf of the Clubs and the UFL.

Section 6. Public Statements:

The UFLPA and the Management Council agree that each will use its best efforts to curtail public comments by Club personnel or players which express criticism of any club, its coach, or its operation and policy, or which tend to cast discredit upon a Club, a player, or any other person involved in the operation of a Club, the UFL, the Management Council, or the UFLPA.

UFL PLAYER'S CONTRACT (Appendix C)

4. PUBLICITY AND UFLPA GROUP LICENSING PROGRAM.

(a)   Player grants to Club and the League, separately and together, the authority to use his name and picture for publicity and the promotion of UFL Football, the League or any of its member clubs in newspapers, magazines, motion pictures, game programs and roster manuals, broadcasts and telecasts, and all other publicity and advertising media, provided such publicity and promotion does not constitute an endorsement by Player of a commercial product. Player will cooperate with the news media, and will participate upon request in reasonable activities to promote the Club and the League.

(b)   Player hereby assigns to the UFLPA and its licensing affiliates, if any, the exclusive right to use and to grant to persons, firms, or corporations (collectively "licensees") the right to use his name, signature facsimile, voice, picture, photograph, likeness, and/or biographical information (collectively "image") in group licensing programs. Group licensing programs are defined as those licensing programs in which a licensee utilizes a total of six (6) or more UFL player images on or in conjunction with products (including, but not limited to, trading cards, clothing, videogames, computer games, collectibles, internet sites, fantasy games, etc.) that are sold at retail or used as promotional or premium items. Player retains the right to grant permission to a licensee to utilize his image if that licensee is not concurrently utilizing the images of five (5) or more other UFL players on products that are sold at retail or are used as promotional or premium items.

ARTICLE XLIV

The League may also conduct random testing for steroids as in the past seasons, but with limits on the number of times any given player can be tested to be negotiated between the Commissioner and the UFLPA.

Section 6. Substance Abuse:

(a)   **General Policy.** The parties agree that substance abuse and the use of anabolic steroids are unacceptable within the UFL, and that it is the responsibility of the parties to deter and detect substance abuse and steroid use and to offer programs of intervention, rehabilitation, and support to players who have substance abuse problems.

(b) **Anabolic Steroids and Related Substances.** The League's existing Policy and Procedure with respect to Anabolic Steroids and Related Substances will remain in effect, except as it may be modified in the future due to scientific advances with respect to testing techniques or other matters. The parties will establish a joint Advisory Committee, consisting of the League's Advisor for Anabolic Steroids and Related Substances and an equal number of members appointed by the UFLPA and by the Management Council, to study pertinent scientific and medical issues and to advise the parties on such matters.

(c) **Drugs of Abuse and Alcohol.** The League's existing Policy and Procedure with respect to Drugs of Abuse and Alcohol will remain in effect, including annual pre-season testing of all players; provided that the parties will promptly make their best efforts jointly to formulate and implement a modified program with respect to Drugs of Abuse and Alcohol to become effective for the 1993 UFL season.

Owners are obligated to notify players 48 hours before conducting a mandatory drug test.

Non-random drug testing is only allowed in the event of an injury.

Non-positive drug violations are treated as if the player has tested positive for a banned substance.

15. INTEGRITY OF GAME. Player recognizes the detriment to the League and professional football that would result from impairment of public confidence in the honest and orderly conduct of UFL games or the integrity and good character of UFL players. Player therefore acknowledges his awareness that if he accepts a bribe or agrees to throw or fix an UFL game; fails to promptly report a bribe offer or an attempt to throw or fix an UFL game; bets on an UFL game; knowingly associates with gamblers or gambling activity; uses or provides other players with stimulants or other drugs for the purpose of attempting to enhance on-field performance; or is guilty of any other form of conduct reasonably judged by the League Commissioner to be detrimental to the League or professional football, the Commissioner will have the right, but only after giving Player the opportunity for a hearing at which he may be represented by counsel of his choice, to fine Player in a reasonable amount; to suspend Player for a period certain or indefinitely; and/or to terminate this contract.